THE
HORSEMAN'S
ETIQUETTE
BOOK

Also by Marcia S. Copper

TAKE CARE OF YOUR HORSE

THE HORSEMAN'S ETIQUETTE BOOK

Marcia S. Copper

Charles Scribner's Sons · New York

DRAWINGS BY CRAIG M. COPPER

Copyright © 1976 Marcia S. Copper

LIBRARY OF CONGRESS CATALOGING IN PUBLICATION DATA
Copper, Marcia S
The horseman's etiquette book.
    Includes index.
    1. Horsemanship. 2. Horsemanship—Etiquette.
I. Title.
SF309.C67   798'.23   76–880
ISBN 0–684–14646–0

1 3 5 7 9 11 13 15 17 19 H/C 20 18 16 14 12 10 8 6 4 2

*A special salute
to a lost friend, Bill Bryan,
who instilled in me a
great respect for any and every
style of riding and,
in particular, for the horse.*

Contents

Foreword

WHY, you may ask, a book about horse manners and riding etiquette? Horseback riding is supposed to be fun! Why should anyone have to bother with "do's and don'ts" and "correct" riding attire?

There is a reason. A very good one. Riding is not only a science; it's an art. Tradition and, yes, riding etiquette are important because they, interwoven with a rider's skill, are what give the sport much of its beauty. No one is born knowing how to ride a horse with style and flair. We must learn. "Do's and don'ts" and "correct" riding attire are a part of what riding is all about.

Of course times have changed. No longer are people confined to their own backyard and the familiarity of their own setting. Today many people are traveling from one end of the country to the other and, in many cases, their horses go too. Obviously those who know basically what is expected of them, those who are aware of the dress being worn, those who make an effort to understand the language spoken are the ones who are accepted much more readily than those who are ignorant of such things.

It is true, also, that more and more people are turning to the horse for pleasure. Unfortunately, and through no fault of their own, many do not have the benefits of the knowledge and training that at one time were automatically passed on from generation to generation in riding families. Although riding schools and horse magazines do an excellent job of informing interested horse people, it is virtually impossible for them to reach all of our vast riding population.

Therefore, for those who love the horse and for those who want to preserve riding sport in its finest form, I submit this book. I am well aware that riding customs and people vary from county to county, state to state, and country to country. But basically, riding etiquette remains the same. When it doesn't—I shall try to warn you of the variations.

At the same time, there is no doubt that the rider who cares need never be afraid to enter the horse world. Common sense, a "do unto others" approach, attention to riding skills, and a genuine respect for the horse will never fail . . . not in any horse society.

THE
HORSEMAN'S
ETIQUETTE
BOOK

1

ᶜHorse Sense

The horse has always captured man's imagination. The Greeks gave him wings. Authors and poets have romanticized him. Why? Because there is an aesthetic quality about the horse that is found in no other animal. Even the "old gray mare" that lives on the farm down the road retains a certain beauty, bony and plagued with arthritis though she may now be. She continues to be loved and cared for, not only for herself as she is today but for the use and pleasure she gave the family in her younger days.

Horsemen have always searched for and will continue to search for that perfect relationship, the successful blending of personality of both horse and rider. Alexander the Great and his horse Bucephalus, General Lee and Traveller, Roy Rogers and Trigger are only a few examples. That special relationship is not easy to find, as each horse is as much of a character as the person who owns him. It's only natural that the horse one person likes and enjoys riding is not necessarily the horse another will like or even feel comfortable upon. I have seen top riders suddenly come face to face with a horse that simply won't respond to them, skilled though they may be. Our Quarter Horse, Sam, came to us for this very reason. His past owners had always found him to be a quiet, gentle horse—so much so, that they had hoped eventually to use him as a guest horse. But it soon became evident that Sam had other ideas. He fought his riders. He would not stand still. He reared for no good reason. He even tried to run away. He was offered to us because I had helped exercise him and because he had always appeared happy and well-behaved when he visited our barn. And, sure enough, the rearing, runaway habits he developed disappeared as soon as he arrived. Only the old, familiar "Casual Sam," as I had named him, remained. I suppose we'll never understand why these things happen; they just do.

It is also a fact that when man does find the horse of his choice, he feels a pride in his animal that is rarely matched except perhaps by a parent's pride in his children. So take heed! Be careful when asked to appraise another's horse. What the owner really wants is an affirmation of his own opinion, not your criticism. Overlook the Roman nose or the pigeon toes and look for the good points. "Kind eyes" is always an excellent answer if you really can't think of anything else to say. "Nice disposition" works too. A friend of mine insists that horses, like babies, are there only to be admired. For no matter how red, crinkly, or cross-eyed that baby may be, he is still beautiful to those who love him. And who would dare tell his parents otherwise? Not I!

Riding is one of the few sports we can enjoy forever. Most horses, bless them, put up with our inadequacies, and as we grow older our infirmities, with tolerance and good humor. It is always beautiful to see horses put long-forgotten smiles back on the faces of mentally and physically handi-capped children. In fact, today there are many programs throughout the country combining horses and children because the children have re-sponded so well.

My own horses kindly put up with my bad back and the odd positions I sometimes have to resort to in order to continue riding. For me, there are times when sitting upright in the saddle is very painful. And one leg has lost much of its strength. To compensate for this, I lean forward and at times even support myself on the horse's neck. Not exactly the best riding position, and certainly not one that I would recommend, but it can be done. One way or another I can continue with the sport I love.

Because of the horse's estimable qualities, some defined and some undefinable, an unwritten riding code was formulated long ago and passed down from one generation of riders to the next. It was devised by horsemen who knew, loved, and respected the horse.

Of prime importance was the first law of any horseman worthy of the title: "Think of your horse's comfort first, then worry about yourself. The horse must depend upon you."

I know of several adoring parents whose children have arrived home from a winter's ride absolutely freezing. But those same children are not allowed to enter the house until they have settled their horses comfortably in their stalls. Then and only then are they allowed in the house to take care of their own needs. The children are learning just as their parents had learned in the past.

Of course this unwritten law stemmed, too, from the fact that in the early days there was no form of transportation for business or social pleasures except the horse. A great deal of effort had to be made to keep him as healthy as possible. After all, if a horse became lame, his owner was suddenly caught with no means of transportation but his own two feet.

The horse is just as dependent upon us today for his health and well-being as he was in days gone by. And although we no longer rely upon the horse for our daily transportation, our riding pleasure is nil when our horse must remain in his stall because he is lame or sick. The first law of horsemen remains: "Think of your horse first."

Safety rules are as necessary to the sport of riding as they are to everyday living. Accidents will occur. At the very least, the falls we take cause bumps and bruises. And we might as well face it, everyone is bound to take a spill sooner or later—that's simply the law of averages. There is an old saying that the rider who is dumped owns the land upon which he falls. Don't I wish it were so! I know I personally would own some of the most beautiful real estate in this country. And I have a few friends who would own a piece of England, Ireland, and Scotland, too.

So, what are some of the basic rules? The "do's and don'ts" of the horse world? Let's start at the beginning.

THE APPROACH AND WORKING AROUND HORSES

It may seem strange to include a segment on approaching and working around horses when writing a book essentially on riding etiquette, but horses take a great deal of care. Sometimes it's necessary to spend as much time or more grooming and preparing the animal for a ride than it takes to ride him. A good horseman knows how to behave correctly around his horse.

Humans rarely create disorder and confusion when they are startled. A horse, on the other hand, has 1,500 pounds on us and can easily do both in a very short amount of time. Horses are sensitive to noise and automatically respond to it. Their first response when frightened is to jump, possibly knocking aside everything in their way (including you). A horse's second reaction, and both reactions may occur almost simultaneously, is to defend himself. He may kick out in any direction.

There is an obvious conclusion. A quiet voice and quiet actions are the rule when entering any stable and when working around horses. Do your best to persuade others to be quiet, too. I have a friend who broke her arm while braiding a horse's mane. The horse knew she was there but he still reacted when a group of noisy children ran into the stable.

But do speak when approaching a horse. Horses have the ability to lock their knees and sleep while standing. They may be completely unaware of a person's approach. A horse's instinct is to react first and think later. It's best to let him know you are there.

Approach a horse from the front whenever possible. If he must be approached from the rear, speak first and then place a hand on his rump so he'll know you're there. Don't stand four feet away and then lean over gingerly to touch him with your fingertips. This is the time to be bold.

Contrary to what many people believe, the closer a person stands to a horse, the less likely it is the horse will kick. Or, if he does, the full power of the blow will be blunted. Most horses raise their tails before they kick. Horsemen have learned to press close to the horse's hindquarters and, if necessary, to put one hand on the tail and hold it down to keep him from kicking. Sounds silly, but it works. Respect a horse's size but know, too, that he will usually accept quiet authority.

LEADING

The left side of the horse is called the *near* side. The right side is called the *off*. Generally horses are led from the near side. This, of course, is a vestige of the past, as men in earlier times carried their weapons on the left side of their bodies. It was more sensible and a great deal easier for a "cavalier" to keep his body between his weapon and his horse for then there was no chance that the two might become "intertwined."

Even a small child can lead a horse if he walks beside his horse's head facing in the direction he and his horse are going, if he does not look back at his horse, and if his walk is sure. I know it's hard to believe, but chances are slim that his heels will be stepped on even though he is a small child. The average horse will keep pace with him. If the horse does seem too eager, a few downward yanks on the bridle or lead shank will usually be enough to remind him to mind his manners.

If the horse is bridled, hold the reins in both hands, the right hand secure under the horse's chin, the left hand holding the remaining length of rein. Horses have the ability to see two different things at the same time. Sometimes this confuses them and they react by shying (swerving or jumping away from the person leading them). If you hold the reins in both hands, there will be very little chance that the horse will escape. The hold under the chin may be released as he jumps away from you, but you still have the rest of the rein in your other hand.

We humans seem to have an innate desire to see our own characteristics in animals we love. In many cases we credit our horses with much more sense than they really have. Horses are not stupid but their capacity to reason or to understand orders is definitely not on a par with ours. Take, for instance, the loving owner who removes saddle and bridle and then says in a sweet voice, "Now, Blackie, stay there while I hang these up." Well, Blackie *may* stand there if the spirit moves him or he may not. He does not *know* he is supposed to remain in one spot, especially if you leave him. A horse is not a dog. He is a special animal with special characteristics and he should be treated as such. Never leave a horse to stand by himself.

MOUNTING AND DISMOUNTING

Riders mount and dismount from the near side of the horse. Again the reason stems from the sword that might interfere. It was more practical to mount with the left foot placed first in the stirrup, leaving the right (sword-free) leg to swing over the saddle. The correct way for any rider to mount is to place the left hand on the horse's withers, the bony lump at the bottom of the neck. The left hand also holds the reins. The right hand is placed either on the pommel of the saddle or, if the rider prefers, right below the pommel. Don't feel odd if you're a beginner and have to make several tries before finally landing in the saddle. It *is* a long way up and there's not one of us who didn't have difficulty mounting when we first started riding (no matter what your riding instructor claims—horse stories are sometimes as exaggerated as fish stories). Feel confident, too, that if you've remembered to tighten the cinch/girth, you won't hurt the horse with your struggles and the saddle will not fall off. I promise.

Horses have always had a tendency to respond to continuity. Therefore, although swords have disappeared from the attire, it has been simpler for horsemen to continue training horses to be mounted from the left. This does not mean that horses cannot be mounted from the right side. Many can. And many horses are trained to accept a rider from either side. But those who ride feel it's easier to continue to use the same practice with every horse, especially a strange horse. Some horses are not as easy to mount as others.

When dismounting, the left foot remains in the stirrup until the right foot is swung over the back of the saddle and joins it. Then the rider may step down from his horse, or preferably, he will remove his left foot from the stirrup and, with both feet free, hop down. There is no danger of a foot being caught in the stirrup when both feet are released first. Western riders are more likely to use the step-down dismounting procedure than English riders, who usually release both feet before dismounting. This is understandable, as the western stirrup is larger than its English counterpart. The western boot is narrower than its English counterpart, too.

"WALK THE FIRST AND LAST MILE"

This is a major rule of horsemanship. Too often it is an unspoken rule that horsemen automatically expect of others. However, there are many riders who don't know or understand the rule and therefore manage to get themselves and their horses in lots of trouble. But if you stop and think for a moment, it really does make good sense. Every horse needs time to limber up just as every athlete requires time to limber up before performing. The person who gives his horse time at the beginning of a ride to loosen his joints and become accustomed to the saddle and the extra weight will have a far more pleasant ride upon a horse more willing to accept his rider. Walk at least five or ten minutes.

Walking is especially important at the end of a ride because it gives the horse time to relax and "cool out" while still moving. Horses are prone to chills and other upsets when they are overheated and left to stand. Thoughtless riders who return to stables on hot, sweating horses are not respected, no matter who they are, king or peasant! It is, and always will be, the rider's responsibility to walk his horse or to see that he is walked as long as necessary until he is cool.

Sometimes, of course, there is no opportunity or time for a rider to "walk a mile" while still in the saddle. Then it is his responsibility to see that his horse is led from the ground until his chest feels cool to the touch. Don't always expect a stable groom to do it for you. *You* do it. The chest is always the last to cool. When the saddle is removed, the horse is briskly rubbed where the saddle has been to improve circulation. If the horse is very hot and the air cool, you should put on a cooler (a form of sweat-blanket for horses). Common sense dictates when it is needed. Horses do not necessarily have to be babied but riders should be aware of their weaknesses and act accordingly.

PACE REGULATION

Obviously it's more exciting to gallop than to walk. Children are notorious "rough riders" who love to play cowboy. A good canter or gallop through the woods or in an open field is exhilaration for us all, and most horses love it as much as we. *But,* every rider, whether he is riding for pleasure or for show, should know that his horse is not a machine. Every horse gets tired and he needs and enjoys a change of pace. A galloping horse must walk from time to time. A trot, a walk, a canter, interspersed here and there add extra variety. Regulating the pace ensures that our horses will not become overtired or strained from their exertions. Any time a horse is asked to exert himself for any reason, he should have the necessary conditioning and training behind him. Any owner who does less is dealing in cruelty to animals and quickly loses the respect of all other horse owners.

It is also true that a trot or a canter in the same place each day soon becomes a habit to the horse and he may be upset if his rider suddenly wishes to change the routine. We used to have a mare whose previous owner had either taught or allowed her to gallop down every hill she met. The unfortunate result when we acquired her was a tremendous fight at each hill. I don't happen to like galloping down steep hills! We never did completely cure her of the habit. It got to be a real bore. Don't let it happen in the first place.

Jumping, although great fun for the rider, puts quite a strain on a horse's legs. We must understand a horse's limitations and allow him time to rest. A tired, sore horse becomes balky and can eventually refuse to work. In horseman's language, he "sours." Horses don't like doing the same thing over and over and over again any more than we do. And most of them aren't that keen on jumping. A few jumps may be kind of fun. Many jumps are nothing but a lot of hard work.

Use horse sense. Demand no more than your horse can learn to do or physically perform and you'll achieve one of the greatest thrills riding can provide: the completely responsive, willing horse. There is one extra boon: you'll gain the respect of your peers!

HORSES AND FOOD

Oh, my! The problems that arise because owners think of their horses as "cute" pets, and feel they'll make more of a friend of their horses if they give them treats. To make matters worse, horses love treats, especially apples, sugar, and carrots. Keep your treats for special occasions or, if you must give them regularly, place them in the horse's feed bin. Treats are an excellent way to teach any horse bad manners. Like the child who expects a present every time Grandma comes to visit, the horse begins to expect a treat each and every time anyone appears in his vicinity. Unfortunately he cannot understand that treats are not always available. As a result, the language in a stable becomes loud and violent as stable personnel are bitten continuously by horses searching for goodies. And sadly, children have been knocked to the ground by horses innocently looking for tidbits. All because some owner has delighted in spoiling his horse. Bad manners, whether in horses or children, are difficult to undo and, in the case of the horse, can be dangerous to the unsuspecting.

TACK

Riding equipment is identified as "tack" and is kept in the tack room. Bridles, saddles, and other riding equipment should be kept clean, soft, and pliable. Sometimes it isn't pleasant or convenient to clean tack—I don't like it much either—but it must be done. Dirty, messy tack is unsightly, becomes brittle, and often causes sores as it stiffly rubs against the horse. A good saddle soaping after each ride and a leather preservative applied if you get caught in the rain should prevent any problems. A word of warning: don't apply too much oil. Oil is used mostly to supple new leather and to help it develop a natural luster. Too much oil breaks down leather.

Horsemen like to enhance their horse's own natural beauty. They also like to show how well their horses can perform without a lot of extra equipment. Bright-colored bridles and saddle pads are used only in special circumstances and for particular types of horses, because they do distract the eye from the horse. Similarly, the least amount of equipment with which a rider can successfully ride his horse is the amount of equipment he will prefer to use. (Frankly, it's a horseman's way of showing off his riding ability and the skill of his horse.)

Naturally tack has to be carefully tailored to fit each individual horse and each individual horse's needs. His conformation and your style of riding dictate the kind of saddle he'll need, and his "way of going" dictates the severity of bit he'll need. A strong, hard-to-hold horse will need a more severe bit, whereas the quieter, more sensitive horse will probably go very well in a gentler, "softer" bit.

If you don't know what kind of tack to use, don't be afraid to ask questions or to experiment. There are excellent books written on the subject of fitting and adjustment of tack. A good professional horseman is an excellent help also. A rule of thumb: start with the gentle bit first.

ATTIRE

The clothes one wears are a part of one whole picture, a picture which, we hope, will always be pleasing to the eye. The attire, of course, varies depending upon the style of riding and the formality of the occasion, but there is a general rule. Riding clothes should never be so bright and fussy that they distract a spectator's attention from the horse. Slim, tailored, quiet-colored attire is always acceptable and very practical. Naturally, long hair should be neatly and appropriately contained. Aside from spoiling a pretty picture, flying hair obstructs the rider's view and distracts the rider when he should be concentrating only upon his horse, where he and his horse are going, and upon his instructor if he is having a lesson.

Chewing gum in public is equally unattractive, especially in the show ring. And I've known not a few riders who have swallowed their gum by mistake and have ended up choking on it. Serves them right!

HORSES AND DISEASE

Horses are as susceptible to infectious disease as humans. And, just as conscientious people place a self-enforced quarantine upon themselves or their family when they are ill, so should a horse owner place a quarantine upon his horse if he suspects his horse is ill. Unfortunately, I have seen sick horses enter the show ring and proceed to infect all the other horses entered. We all want to knock out our competition—but not that way! Preventive shots for many infectious diseases are available from veterinarians and they should be used. A sick horse belongs in his own barn until he is well again. This is only good sense and certainly common courtesy.

2

Horse Manners

A well-mannered horse may be defined as a horse willing to stand or execute any ordinary gait his master wishes.

Horse manners are extremely important, for it won't do a rider one whit of good to know what is expected of him if he is mounted on a horse he cannot control. In fact, it's downright embarrassing!

Of course, young and/or inexperienced horses cause problems when they are placed in situations they don't understand. And, I must admit, even in situations they do understand. They shy, buck, and pull all kinds of ridiculous stunts. Most riders accept these inconsistencies with understanding and good humor and do their best to help their horses overcome their fears, excitement, and tangled feet. At the same time, a wise rider tries to avoid having his horse meet several unusual situations at one time. He'll ride in very small groups at first and, if possible, will ride beside an older, more knowledgeable horse who will give his own horse extra confidence and teach him manners.

But I am concerned here mostly with the horse that is supposedly already trained and knows better. At the top of the list of unmannerly horses is the horse who kicks! Although it is a universal custom to tie a red ribbon in a horse's tail as a warning to others that he kicks, the horse who kicks is still embarrassing to ride and definitely a hindrance in any kind of group situation. Avoid owning a kicking horse if at all possible.

The difficult-to-control horse is another disaster for the average rider. Horsemen sigh when they talk about the horse with only two gaits—slow and fast. This kind of horse is no fun to ride because he takes such concentration that his rider has no time to socialize with friends.

The puller is in this category also. The puller complies with his rider's wishes but only if his rider is strong enough to slow him down solely by brute strength. I don't see any fun in riding if my arms are still suffering the next day from the muscular exertion. I'd rather look for another horse that I could ride comfortably. Extra-strong bitting is not much help with the real puller although there are cases in which an accomplished rider can achieve miracles with retraining.

The rearing horse and the wheeling horse (a horse who spins at most any time for no good reason) are a danger to everyone and should be avoided by all but an accomplished rider. Most times even the accomplished rider won't care to ride them. Horses that buck all the time—not just occasionally from good spirits—are not much fun either. After all, the major purpose of riding is to have fun. Constantly bucking horses belong in a rodeo, not in a pleasure-riding situation. They are not well-mannered.

Be alert if you ride a horse who shies a great deal. He may be telling you that he has eye problems.

Stable manners are equally important. No one likes to work around a horse with poor stable manners. Horses that crowd their grooms against stall walls are decidedly unpopular. Biting and kicking horses should be avoided for obvious reasons.

Another unpopular horse is the one who fights with his neighbors or kicks the sides of his stall, eventually destroying his surroundings. He makes extra work for everyone, not to mention the time, labor, and expense necessary to repair the stall.

Many nervous horses develop bad habits in their stalls. Cribbing (chewing and sucking on the sides of their stalls) and weaving (rocking from side to side as they stand in their stalls) are two prime examples. But although they are unpleasant vices, they are not dangerous to the people working around them. They can be tolerated. And there are devices that prevent, or at least diminish, some bad habits.

Another source of frustration is the horse who will not load into a horse trailer or van. The young or inexperienced horse can be taught, but there are others who, for no reason that you know of anyway, will fight loading for hours on end. Avoid that sort of horse, for he will cause more disappointment and ruin more anticipated rides than you can imagine. Our Flicka was just such a pony. One time, because she was so nasty to load, we arrived two hours late to a horse show that we had all looked forward to. Much as I loved her, at that moment I could have killed her. The problem was solved quickly on the return trip. Two strong men literally picked her up and put her in the trailer. She was in before she knew what happened. Unfortunately, there are not always two strong men around to help.

The kindly, well-mannered horse inspires more confidence and enthusiasm in his rider than any of these ill-mannered demons ever could.

The Basic Position
- ~ western jog
~ gaited trot
~ posting trot

3

Basic Riding Position

It is interesting that throughout recorded history so little about the horse has changed. Even riding style has remained basically the same: in simple terms, we must keep our balance or we land on the ground! The basic style is simply adapted to the type of horse we happen to be riding and the use for which he is intended.

Part of the joy of riding is trying new things. The hunt seat, saddleseat, or dressage rider wants to go on a pack trip or even try his hand at herding cattle if he's skillful enough. The western rider moves to a new area and finds himself an alien in fox-hunting country. It's an odd experience to change horses and styles of riding, but not nearly as difficult as you might believe. Not too long ago I met a young man who had been brought up on a cattle ranch in Montana. He came East to college and within a year was doing a fair amount of successful steeplechasing (horse racing over fences). Now there's a switch for you! Of course there's no reason on earth why you and I need make such a dramatic switch, but he certainly proved it can be done.

Naturally, few people today are proficient in all types of riding. Each form takes special practice and concentration. Don't expect miracles when you visit new areas. You can be more confident if you admit your inexperience, for then the chances are excellent that you will be mounted on an animal that will forgive your ignorance. I'm sure your host doesn't want you in a difficult situation any more than you want to be in one. And really, with a little explanation from the expert in the area, you will probably do quite well, especially if you have taken it upon yourself, as my young friend did, to learn the basics of riding posture.

The natural aids a rider uses to maneuver his horse are his hands, legs, weight, and sometimes voice. Correct placement of each of the aids is important, for they are the rider's means of control. Our hands steer the horse, our legs make him go forward, backward, or sideways, and our weight is distributed to help him perform more easily.

What is good riding posture?

The rider at the halt is expected to sit straight in his saddle. His upper arms rest quietly at his sides. An observer, when viewing horse and rider, should see a straight line running from the rider's elbow—to the hands— through the reins—to the horse's mouth. This way light but firm contact is achieved; in other words, the horse is sensitive to his rider's demands upon the reins but he is not hurt by those demands.

The rider's back should be held straight but not stiff. A rounded back or a hollowed back are common errors.

The leg falls directly under the body with the knee bent just enough to keep the rider from losing his balance. Too long or too short a stirrup may cause cramps in the leg and always forces the torso into an unnatural position.

The foot and the ankle are relaxed. The toe is pointed forward but not too far in or out to place the rider in an uncomfortable position. One way to tell if your foot is in correct position is to look down over your knee. If you can see more than the very tip of your boot, your leg is too far forward. If you can't see any of your boot, your leg is too far back. There should be a straight vertical line between the point of the knee and the toe.

The overall picture achieved is one of continuity and fluidity, neither

Grazing livestock are not in a field or on the range for your roundup pleasure. If you must ride through pasture land, ride through quietly and leave the livestock as peaceful as you found them.

Picnic rides are a delight. But please, trash belongs with the rider until it can be placed in a proper receptacle. It is always disagreeable to find cans, bottles, or gum wrappers along trails, and broken glass is always a danger to the horse. Cigarettes and cigars are potential fire hazards. They must be carefully stubbed out. Use the bottom of your boot if nothing else is available.

Any fire must be carefully tended, and all embers should be generously doused and covered with dirt before you leave the picnic site. I encountered a wall of fire out in the woods one day. It was an appalling experience, one I hope never to have again.

Voices tend to carry in the country much more than you realize. Keep your voice down if you are riding near someone's house. I myself have heard private conversations I had no business hearing and I have heard grossly unpleasant language that I never care to hear. I resent every minute of it!

Our family has always enjoyed trail riding with our family pets. Our Great Dane, Rebel; our two mutts, Penny and Twinkle; and even our cat, Tigger (he thinks he's a dog), are always eager to join us. But we never allow them to do so unless we are riding on our own property. There are two reasons for this: one, the rider is unwittingly introducing his dog to new territory and thus is encouraging him to wander; and two, country dogs are possessive of their own property. They resent having another dog on their territory, and they will fight to keep him off. Don't ride cross-country with your pets.

5

Group Riding

Suppose the local riding group has invited you to join them for one of their Sunday rides. You've heard of the fun that they have and can't wait for Sunday to come. But now that you've accepted the invitation you're getting cold feet. You don't know exactly what is expected of you and your horse when riding in a group. What if you do something wrong? Well, don't despair. There are a few rules to remember, but mostly, just be yourself and be courteous.

The most important rule when riding in a group is *to keep your distance*. At a walk, a horse's length apart is the correct measure. Anyone who rides closer is asking to be kicked. Even horses that are not known to kick may do so if they are run up on or crowded. Furthermore, the rider on the horse in front is not very happy either when his horse's heels are stepped on. He may end up with a lame horse as a result of your lack of courtesy.

If the group you join likes to "move on," remember that fast-moving horses cover a great deal of ground in a very short time, so judge your distance by the speed at which your horse is moving. I suggest one and a half to two horse's lengths apart at the trot; three lengths apart at the canter. If the group is jumping fences, be extra careful and stay at least four horse's lengths apart. Then, if the rider in front falls or if his horse refuses the jump, you will have enough distance between you to allow time to pull up and avoid what could be a disastrous collision.

The rider with a horse who continuously refuses jumps should move to the rear of the group in order to allow the group to move on at a more even pace. And really, if your horse refuses *that* many jumps, I suggest you get yourself another horse or forget about riding where there are fences.

There will always be a time when someone in the group will have to dismount, sometimes to open a gate, sometimes to clear a trail, or sometimes just to retrieve something. Nothing is more difficult than trying to mount a horse when every other horse is leaving the immediate vicinity. Horses gain confidence from one another and, if they have the choice, prefer to be together. So check to make sure that at least one horse remains behind to give the other horse assurance until the rider on the ground is once more secure in his saddle. (You'll earn extra bonus points if you are the one to remain behind.)

The cavalry used to use hand signals to ensure better group discipline. The hand straight up meant slow down or walk; the fist up twice meant trot; the fist up three times meant canter. The hand pointed toward the ground left or right meant possible danger in that direction, such as a hole in the ground, wire, barbed wire, and so on. Hand signals are rarely used today, but when they are they help immeasurably. It is such a pleasure, especially when riding single file on a trail, to know what is going to happen *before* it happens.

The courteous rider watches not only his own horse but also for any injury to the horses in front of him. A pulled shoe or a cut on the hindquarters is very difficult for the rider on top of the injured horse to see. I shall always be grateful to the person who called my attention to a hind shoe pulled halfway off and pointing dangerously at Sam's other hind leg. If we had continued on, Sam might have sustained a serious injury. Of course, we removed the shoe immediately, using the stirrup as a tool, and that was the end of the problem.

All riders in a group should travel no faster than the poorest rider in the group can safely manage. And, if the horses are traveling in single file, be extra careful. There is always a crack-the-whip effect when riding single file. Give the rear horse and rider time every now and then to catch their breath. I've been the back-up rider many times. In every case it's been fortunate that I've been riding a "fit" horse, for I've done many a gallop only to discover later that my leader had never gone any faster than a trot.

Courtesy on horseback is in some ways quite different from courtesy on the ground. For instance, riders in the saddle rarely shake hands. They nod their heads or a gentleman may doff his hat, but a separation is always maintained between his horse and yours. Horsemen learned a long time ago that not every horse is automatically a friendly horse.

Do not hold low branches for the rider behind you. It's very thoughtful but the time element is such that it is almost impossible not to end up simply snapping them back into his face. Each rider must bend down and go through on his own.

If you see another group of riders, approach it quietly. Many horses catch the excitement of a new arrival and react accordingly, especially if the newcomers arrive at a gallop. The same applies to the rider who leaves a group.

Don't hold up a group of riders. If you wish to water your horse, adjust your saddle, take a picture, or whatever, pull out of line and allow the others to pass. Don't expect them to stay with you.

And most important! Don't play jokes when aboard a horse. They may backfire, for although humans understand jokes, the horses usually don't. The latest "joke" I saw ended with the unsuspecting rider hospitalized with a broken collarbone. Have fun, but don't play foolish games.

Most states insist that riders using roads remain together in a group and travel with the flow of traffic. If an accident does occur and horse and rider have not obeyed the law, court action could result.

If you and your friends plan a moonlight ride, make sure the moon is full (not just for romance but so the horses can *see*) and plan the ride cross-country. Traveling on roads at night is just plain foolish. Just recently I heard about two riders taking an evening ride. One horse was on one side of the road, the other horse on the opposite side. A car came along and the driver, seeing the horse on his side of the road, pulled way over to avoid it. Unfortunately, the driver didn't see the horse on the other side until it was too late. The rider fell through the windshield, the horse was badly hurt, and the car was a mess! Need I say more?

6

Terrain

Whether you're off for the day or for a few weeks, you must know how to read your terrain and ride correctly over and through it. The best thing I can advise is that you be mounted on a horse that knows his country. I've seen beautiful show hunters trip over roots on a trail and fret at each bush and stream they meet. Their kingdom is the show ring and noisy horse-show surroundings. Similarly, I've seen trail horses that could take Grand Canyon like a pro balk and express real panic in the schooling atmosphere of a show stable. Each area of the country is different and has its own peculiarities. If you must ride your own horse in a new area, ride him slowly and carefully at first until he learns to adapt. At the same time, learn to help your horse to help himself.

Hard ground is always a potential hazard to your horse's legs. They are the most sensitive part of his body and constant hard riding on hard ground is sure to make him lame. Always walk on paved roads. Not only is the pavement hard but paved roads are inclined to be slippery.

Deep sand can be found most anywhere, not just at the beach. And make no mistake, sand is just as wearing for a horse to travel through as it is for a human.

Bogs are foolers and sometimes not easily recognized. If you see an area that seems muddy or slightly damp on top, take care. Mud has a tendency to pull. I've lost a few of my own shoes walking through the stuff; the same thing can happen to your horse. Bogs strain a horse's legs, too. Sometimes a bog is deeper than it appears to be. If possible, test the footing before going through. If there are many horses, sometimes more than one path must be made. Bogs which are not too deep at first can get much worse after a number of horses pass through.

Water crossings are fun and can be a challenge. Small streams and quiet rivers are no problem except that we must watch for slippery rocks and/or sharp stones that could bruise the horse's feet. An alert rider will have no difficulty. But look out! Horses, especially on warm days, love to fold their legs and roll in an inviting stream, regardless of who or what may be upon their backs. Always keep a firm hold on the reins and urge a horse forward with your legs when traveling through water. If he starts to paw with his front feet, don't worry about your manners. Pull up on the reins and holler and kick. Do anything you can think of to get that horse out of the water, or you may end up sopping wet with one very messy saddle. I had my first water drenching in a Missouri river. I'll never forget the shock of the cold water or the laughter of my companions. Fortunately the bottom was sandy, and horse, rider, and saddle were unscathed. Nothing was really damaged but my ego, and that got a solid trouncing!

Swift water is tricky. A horse should cross facing slightly upstream. Don't watch the water on the downstream side. For some odd reason it can mesmerize you and some riders actually fall into the water.

Many years ago I taught riding at a camp in Vermont. Sometimes when the weather was really hot, we'd take the horses for a swim in the lake, which they really enjoyed and so did we. Of course this was a planned swim, so the horses wore only a halter and a lead shank. But sometimes on a trail ride there is no way to continue the ride without going through the water, saddles, bridles, riders, and all. Try to remember a few basic rules, if you must swim. (1) You must get off your horse. (2) The reins should be as loose as possible. (3) The reins should not be tied or sewed together. A swimming horse reaches out with his head and his front feet, and he might get his feet caught in the reins and drown. It *has* happened! (4) No rider should swim in front of his horse. Instead, hold on to the saddle on the downstream side or hang on to his tail. Don't get in front of his feet. (5) Try to keep plenty of room between your horse and the horse in front of you or your horse may try to use the front horse as a life raft. (6) Be prepared to mount as soon as your horse finds firm ground. He'll want to get out of there as quickly as possible.

Every trail rider will on occasion come across some sort of obstacle that scares the wits out of his horse. Clumps of bushes harbor all sorts of horrors for horses. And, you know, they may be right. I'll never forget the time Scott and I were out beagling. We were standing very quietly next to a pile of brush when out of the blue it said, "Gobble, Gobble!" Talk about horses! That crazy turkey scared the wits out of *us!* We never did see it. Horses may know something we don't know. Do respect their caution.

At other times, the going may look dangerous even though the horse is not frightened. Each situation must be judged carefully. Don't be ashamed to get off and lead your horse if you think it's necessary.

Mountains can be found east, north, west, and south. It is best to go directly up and directly down steep but fairly short inclines. This way the horse is better able to gather his feet directly underneath him and to keep his balance. Unless there is a trail, going across a steep hill is much more difficult for him and balance is precarious.

Rocks are nasty and must be ridden over carefully. They are slippery and any horse can stumble. In really mountainous country, rock slides are a possibility too. Slow and careful riding is essential. Shout a warning to those in front of you if a rock slide should start and then look for a place that might be safe for you and your horse until the slide is over.

Most important of all, a horse that is tired is not reliable and definitely not safe. Remember, no matter where you are, your horse is doing most of the work. Give him plenty of time to rest.

7

Trail-Riding Competition

There are three kinds of trail riding that riders participate in competitively. (1) The *pleasure ride* is a fairly easy trail ride over a prescribed course to be completed within a certain amount of time; the distance is not great, no real training is necessary, and it's a fun way to "learn the ropes" before entering into the much more difficult (2) *endurance ride* or (3) *competitive trail ride.*

In an endurance ride, the first horse to finish in decent physical condition is proclaimed the winner. Many of the rides are a hundred miles long and must be completed within twenty-four hours. Everyone who finishes within the time allowed is presented with an award, for the ride is always difficult. Not every horse has the stamina and the ability to complete the course. Qualified veterinarians are stationed at checkpoints along the way to make sure that the horse (or mule—they're allowed too) is physically able to continue. The endurance ride is a test of the rider, too. He must know how his horse responds both physically and mentally to different terrain. Naturally, long-distance riding requires stops along the way for rest, feed, and water. Everything must be taken into consideration. A well-thought-out ride plan is a necessity, and that takes skill.

Competitive trail riding has aspects of both pleasure and endurance rides. As in the other two, there is a special route and the horse's physical condition, pulse, respiration, and so forth are checked at intervals. However, instead of being judged only upon his ability to continue, the horse is scored on his fitness at each checkpoint. The score accumulates throughout the ride. There is a maximum and a minimum time allowed and points are taken off for everyone whose time is outside that range. The judge's committee determines before the ride begins the ideal time in which the ride can be completed. The competitors are not informed of this time. It is up to each one individually to figure out what he believes the best time should be. Therefore, it's not always the horse who completes the ride in the fastest time who wins. It is the horse who completes the ride closest to the ideal time. But that's not all! As each *horse* is judged and scored for his condition, soundness, way of going, and manners, each *rider* is judged upon grooming, equitation, tack and equipment, trail care, trail safety, courtesy, and stabling. The final overall winner of a competitive trail ride has every reason to be proud. He's done his homework and he knows his horse.

In each kind of ride there are different divisions and degrees of difficulty. Any type horse can enter unless specifications stipulate otherwise. Saddle horses, western horses, hunters . . . it doesn't matter. What does matter is how successfully each horse responds on the trail.

Don't let your boyfriend, girlfriend, or *anyone* talk you into entering anything but a pleasure ride on the spur of the moment. You'll do neither your horse nor yourself a favor. *Proper conditioning is mandatory.* It won't work, either, if you have friends condition your horse while you're busy elsewhere. *You* must be as fit as your horse or you'll hinder his performance. It's a well-known fact that winded, unfit riders tend to slip and slide all over their horse's backs. Many serious trail riders, to get themselves into better condition, jog, swim, jump rope, and so forth, in addition to spending hours in the saddle.

It won't hurt to do some "test driving." Measure a road or an old, familiar trail from start to finish. Then time the course at the walk, trot, and canter. Talk with your vet and learn how to check your horse's pulse and respiration so you can judge the degree of difficulty your horse has in covering ground. Learn, too, how long it takes for your horse to *recover* from his exertions. Slow walks and trots up and down hills are an excellent way to put a horse into fit condition.

Any kind of tack is allowed as long as it is soft, pliable, and fits your horse comfortably. The same goes for attire. Be neat. Wear well-fitting clothes that don't bind. A long-sleeved shirt to protect your arms from the sun or brush along the trail helps. A hat with a brim will help, too. Don't be short-sighted about your attire. Long-distance trail riding is no joke. Wear boots or shoes that are as comfortable to walk in as they are to ride in, for many trail riders find it necessary to dismount and walk with their horses at times in order to help their horses complete the ride more successfully. It's not uncommon for a rider to dismount and "tail" his horse (follow his horse) up a particularly steep incline. A pair of new boots bought especially for the ride would be a dreadful mistake. Break them in first; it prevents blisters!

Don't forget that, as your horse works progressively harder, he will have to be fed more to stay healthy. Discuss proper diet with friends, professional horsemen, and your vet. Most important, watch your horse and how he responds to the food. He'll tell you better than anyone just how much feed is right or wrong for him. Don't get him too fat. Being overweight can be just as dangerous to him as being underweight.

Pay particular attention to his legs and his feet as you work him and watch for any weakness that might appear. Discuss with your blacksmith the kind of shoe your horse should wear to travel over the countryside. Different terrain requires different kinds of shoes. Do realize, too, that some trail-ride associations specify the kind of shoe your horse may or may not be allowed to wear. Different associations will always have different rules. Learn the rules for each ride you decide to enter and then abide by them.

By this time, if you've prepared yourself and your horse properly, you should be all set to go out and *win!* But either way, win or lose, you'll feel better than you have in ages, probably be a lot slimmer than when you started your physical fitness regime, and best of all, you'll see more beautiful country and experience satisfaction with yourself and your horse that you'll remember always. It makes every bit of the work worthwhile.

8

Ring Etiquette

One surefire way to make friends with people of similar interests is to board your horse in a riding stable. And just as important, the stable's riding arena and/or outdoor ring can be invaluable to any rider who wants to improve the capabilities of his horse. A flat, confined area serves a multitude of training purposes.

Unfortunately it is rare to have the ring to you and your horse alone. We are once more in a group atmosphere. We must share.

Pay attention! There is nothing more annoying than the rider who allows his horse to shove against other horses or who allows his horse to ride up on the heels of another. Usually it happens because the rider is too busy chatting to pay attention to where he's going. I repeat, horses, like people, have their friends and their foes. A good horse's distance behind and a fair width apart should be kept at all times, whether in a ring or on the trail.

Sometimes it seems as though everyone who owns a horse at the stable has decided to ride at the same time. There are horses everywhere! Well, if you have the time, go home and try again later in the day. If you don't have time, go ahead and brave it. You'll find it won't be so bad.

Especially if everyone travels in the same direction. Those riders who wish to move at a faster pace should pass on the inside of the circle. Sometimes there are jump standards or other obstacles in the ring which make passing a little difficult. Then a quiet word to the rider in front whom you are passing on his left or right is usually all that is necessary to avoid running into him. There are always a few mistakes and a few apologies, but on the whole, the system works pretty well.

Horses need to be schooled to travel both directions in the ring, so that they will develop suppleness and a well-rounded athletic ability. Furthermore, all horses get bored and tired going in the same direction all the time, especially those doing ring work. Think about it a bit. Obviously there is much more weight placed on the inside leg as the horse continues in a circle. Try jogging in a small circle yourself. Your inside leg will begin to throb in a short amount of time. One shouldn't expect a horse to react any differently. Don't be too shy to request a reverse from time to time. Most riders will be perfectly willing to oblige. They simply hadn't thought to reverse themselves.

Sooner or later a rider will get dumped. When a rider falls—and this applies not only to the ring but to *almost* every riding situation (hunting is an exception), all riders should halt until the horse is caught and rider and horse are back together. Again, this is only common sense. A loose horse is usually a frightened one. He can cause damage not only to himself by tripping over loose, flapping reins, but he can prompt all kinds of undesirable activity among the other horses. Horses catch both excitement and fear from one another and quickly respond—much to the chagrin and dismay of the other riders who have to work very hard to remain on their own suddenly "spirited" mounts.

For the same reason, a rank (unruly, misbehaving) horse should not be taken into the riding ring with other horses unless you are sure he is welcome. Instead, try to find a time when the ring is unoccupied or when the other horses in the ring are known to be quiet and calm by nature and not likely to be upset by the pranks of a rambunctious horse.

If a class is in session in the ring while you are riding, be silent or speak quietly. Nothing is more distracting than laughter and garbled chatter when one is trying to concentrate or listen for direction from his instructor. The instructor isn't happy either when he is forced to shout to make himself heard above the noise. One full day of shouting and you may lose your instructor for the rest of the week!

9

The Occasional Rider

It's a sin, you scold yourself, to be inside on such a beautiful day! Spring fever, perhaps? You're not sure. All you know is that you feel restless. You'd like to do something different, something unusual. It takes some thought and a lot more pacing but finally the perfect solution comes: horseback riding! At first the thought shakes you up a bit. It's been years since you were last on a horse. The more you think about the idea, though, the better it sounds. You hurry to the phone to suggest that a friend join you (you're not going by yourself!) and then, with your friend's enthusiastic approval, you call the neighborhood stable to make a reservation.

Good for you! You're going about it the right way. Reservations are a help not only to the stable manager but to you, for there is every chance that a horse will not be available for the rider who "pops in" unexpectedly. Make advance reservations whenever possible. Group rides (for more than three) should always be arranged in advance.

Don't worry about clothes. The average rental stable can't be too formal, since it caters to many who ride only four or five times a year and who can't spend a lot of money on riding attire. Of course, it is nice to wear informal attire if you have it. If you don't, a pair of well-fitting but not binding long pants (solid color preferred) and sturdy shoes are the only prerequisites. Be neat. Be tailored. Save the wild colors for the office picnic where they'll be appreciated.

The first question asked of you when you arrive at the stable is what kind of a rider you think you are. Sometimes it's difficult to judge. Most people identify a novice rider as one who knows how to walk, trot, and canter but is not too secure in the saddle. The intermediate rider is much more secure and will not lose his seat if the horse jumps around a little bit. Be honest! Admit you're a beginner or a novice if that is what you are. On the other hand, don't be too modest to admit you can ride well if you know you can. Your frankness helps the stable manager to select the horse equal to your riding ability.

Perhaps you're new in town and the stable is unfamiliar. You arrive only to find it equipped with horses trained quite differently from what you had expected. Don't let that discourage you. Go ahead and ride anyway. New experiences never hurt any of us. Ask the stable manager for help in riding the horse. He'll be glad to tell you enough to get you going. Chances are your horse will be tolerant of your mistakes and you'll have a story to write about to your friends.

Every bit of extra information you can get, whether the riding style is familiar or not, will help to make your ride more pleasant. Ask about the temperament of the horse. Is he the nervous type? Fast moving? Slow? Does he have any special quirks you should look out for? Does he shy at cars? Is he afraid of dogs? The stable might forget to tell you if you don't think to ask.

Every stable runs on a schedule, and most rent horses by the hour. Do call if you think you might run late for your riding date. Your phone call gives the stable an opportunity to adjust its schedule. The horse reserved for you can be put into his stall to wait comfortably for you or he can be used by someone else until you arrive. Keep an eye on the time when you're out riding and limit the ride to an hour if that is the amount of time you have agreed to. Get permission before your ride if you'd like to ride for a longer period. This is only fair. How would *you* like to arrive at the stable at a prearranged time only to find the horse you were scheduled to ride had not yet returned? Half an hour later, you're still waiting. Not much fun!

One other hint. Don't ride for much more than an hour your first time out if you haven't ridden in a while. I guarantee your muscles won't like it.

The rental stable also has an obligation to you. Your horse should look well fed and be neatly groomed. The tack should be clean and carefully put together. It's not necessary that the stable be spotless but aisles should be swept. Stalls shouldn't smell rancid or look as though they had never been cleaned. Miserable-looking stables provide miserable-looking horses, who, in turn, give you a miserable ride. Stay away from that kind of stable. They *deserve* to go out of business—the faster the better!

Stables have rules. The rules are not just for your safety but to protect the stable, too. If you don't see a list posted somewhere, ask for them and then abide by them.

Many stables insist that new riders, regardless of skill, be accompanied by a guide the first few times they ride. The stable isn't insulting your riding ability. The rule was made to protect you. Certainly the guide has an opportunity to assess your trail-riding ability and to assist you with your horse, but you, in turn, have an opportunity to learn firsthand about some of the many trails available. Knowing where you're going is much better than wandering around aimlessly and perhaps getting lost or, even worse, getting you and your horse into situations you can't handle.

There will always be areas within riding range where horses are not allowed. Please help the stable: respect the land over which you do ride and *keep out* of the areas where horses are not allowed. It could mean the difference between your riding stable's remaining in business and being forced to close because riders would not respect the landowner's wishes.

Most important of all, be friendly and polite while riding. Remember you are the stable's representative. Help them to maintain a good reputation.

Help your horse, too. Riders new to the sport are inclined to picture themselves in some sort of romantic scene galloping their horses off into the sunset. I hate to disillusion you, but riding really isn't like that. Cowboy movies are shot in scenes. The horses don't gallop continuously as they appear to do on the screen. The ASPCA would set upon the movie studio immediately if they did. Your rental horse can't gallop continuously either. Remember you're riding a horse that spends many, many hours a day doing his job. Be kind to him. Give him time to rest during your ride and always bring him back to the stable cool, not hot and covered with sweat.

Rental horses are used by a great variety of people and most learn very quickly which rider rides with control and which rider doesn't. Don't be surprised to experience an interesting first fifteen minutes while you and your horse get to know each other. Usually if the horse discovers you mean business and will not tolerate his eating grass, for example, when you want him to walk, he'll give up trying and mind his manners. Don't be mean or harsh. Do be firm. On the other hand, there may be a time when the horse is simply too much for you to handle. Sometimes the stable manager can give you a clue or two that, when applied, make all the difference in the world. Don't be too embarrassed to request another horse if you can't manage the one you have. There is no crime in being afraid. It's important that you find the horse that suits you, for it's only then that you'll gain the confidence you need to enjoy your ride. One pleasurable ride will lead to another and I'll wager that soon our riding sport will have a new member. Welcome.

10

The Western Rider

As a child I spent many happy days in the saddle pretending I was one cowboy hero or another. My horse would gallop across a field with me crouched down on one side of the saddle peeking over his back pretending to shoot at imaginary rustlers. I practiced flying dismounts and running mounts constantly. I landed on my head a lot, too. But my, I had fun.

One cannot help but let the mind wander to cowboys and Indians, buffalo and cattle, settlers and cavalry, when one thinks of western riding —and of course, the western horse. Without him the West would never have been.

Historians are still arguing about how the horse first appeared in the West. Everyone in those days was too busy living to think about recording history. But it is generally conceded that the first horses came with the Spaniards in the South as they crossed over what is now our U.S. border to establish trading posts and missions. It didn't take long for the Indians to realize the value of the horse. Indian raids were frequent and the horses became one of their victory spoils. But then, and I have to chuckle at this, the Indians didn't know how to *ride* the horses once they got them. They discovered, as have we all, that no one is born knowing how to ride. So

47

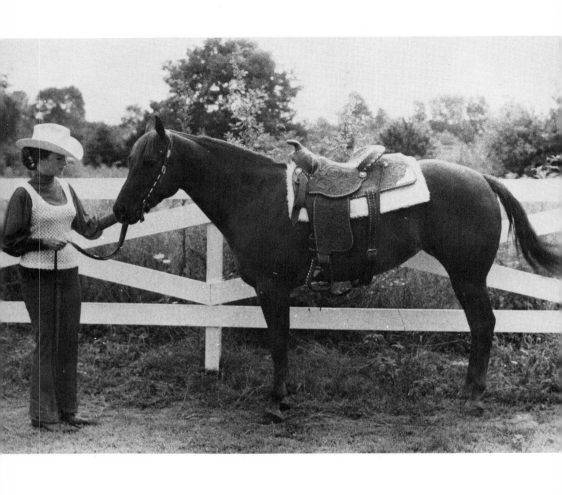

back the Indians went to the Spaniards, this time to watch and learn from them. As a result, many Spanish riding techniques and customs are still in effect in this country today.

As trading posts advanced farther and farther into U.S. territory, horse trading became a profitable business. The horses came farther and farther north and finally reached the Indians in the Northwest. But there well-established French traders who were the Indians' friends became the riding instructors.

This much we believe to be fact. Why? One reason is that the Southwest Indians habitually used the Spanish reata to help control his horseherds. The reata was a rope made from cowhide, closely braided and made flexible by applications of tallow. The Northwest Indians used the French lariat, a loosely braided rope made of buffalo hide. Western riding customs to this day vary because of the different riding instruction given way back then. Things are becoming a little bit easier, though. For instance, today whether the rider carries the French lariat, the Spanish reata, or the lasso, they are *all* called rope.

The horse of the "Old West" wasn't very pretty and he wasn't very large, but he did have his attributes. He was a sturdy beast, nimble of foot, and he possessed great stamina. His conformation was such that he could carry heavy loads for a long period of time before he needed a rest. He was an "easy keeper." He learned to live off of the land he roamed, for when the horses were not in use it was far more practical to turn them out until they were needed again. Naturally only the hardiest, the swiftest, and the most intelligent survived.

The new settlers admired the little western horse and recognized his value but they couldn't help but want a horse possessing more of the refinement that their horses had had in the East. Already the Easterners had bred a fancy horse they called a "quarter horse" because he was skilled in running the quarter mile in astonishing time. The settlers brought him west as they did the Thoroughbred and the Morgan. Thus the horse from the East met the horse from the West and the western horse as we know him today was born. I'm not sure I would want to name a specific breed as being "The Horse of the West" since everyone has a preference. One of the more popular breeds is the American Quarter Horse and he certainly deserves a place in history because he is so adaptable and intelligent. But there are others who claim that the American Saddlebred trained western style is the best, and even others who swear by any one of many other breeds.

The western rider today is a practical rider and he is found riding every kind of horse imaginable. What the rider really wants is a handy, sensible, fairly sturdy horse that can be trained to work. A handy horse turns quickly in balance, scrambles up and down slippery places with ease, does not panic if an unusual situation arises, and is sturdy enough to carry extra equipment or even another man if the occasion demands it. When that type of horse is found, no matter what his breed, he is greatly valued. He is the true western horse.

The western saddle as we know it came into being because men needed a saddle that was comfortable for several hours or even days at a time and that was large enough to carry bed rolls, ropes, fence gear, and/or anything else deemed necessary to daily life.

The western style of riding developed as the style best suited to doing man's work. For example, the western horse was taught to neck rein, to move away from whichever rein leaned on his neck. As only one hand was necessary to neck rein a horse, the rider's other hand was left free to open gates, signal, rope cattle, and so on.

The western horse is noted for his quiet, easy gaits. After all, no one wants to stay all day in the saddle of a horse that is uncomfortable to ride. His walk is free, natural, and quick. His trot is slow. That's why it's called the jog trot. Because it's so easy, the rider has no difficulty sitting to it, and the horse can cover a lot of territory comfortably without tiring himself (the western rider usually does not post to the trot as the English rider does). The lope (a slow, three-beat canter) and the gallop are the western horse's other gaits.

So, if you find yourself in cow country and you're from the big city, relax and enjoy. But do remember that two hands are never used on the reins. You'll only confuse your horse if you try.

The hand holding the reins is carried low and just forward of the saddle horn. The other hand rests on your thigh ready for action. There are some parts of the country where the extra hand is carried in a bent position just as if the rider were holding two reins. It seems a rather unnatural position to me, but it is considered correct in many areas. The right-handed person holds the reins in his left hand, the left-handed person holds his reins in his right hand, to keep his dexterous hand free, remember? Although the horse is trained to move freely on a loose rein, the reins should not be so loose that all contact between the hand and the horse's mouth is lost. Even cutting horses need direction from their riders when they're not performing in a show. The best way to describe "loose" is to say that your reins should be just long enough so that if you pull back behind the horn, the rein is taut; put the hand just forward of the horn and the rein is loose.

Custom in different parts of the country plays a large part in dictating the manner in which the reins are held, too. I don't believe you'll be too far wrong if you hold split reins (reins that are not braided or fastened together in some way) in an open hand. In other words, the hand is relaxed, the reins run over the forefinger across the palm of the hand. The remainder (or bight) of rein lies on the near side of the horse.

But what if the reins are held together by a romal, or are fastened together in some other way? Well, then the rules change. The reins come up through the bottom of the hand and out the top between the thumb and forefinger. Usually the romal hangs down on the near side but there are some areas of the country where the romal is used as a quirt (a whip) and then the remainder of rein is held in the right hand. Remember that the quirt, like the whip, is never used in front of the saddle.

Some people prefer to ride with the index finger between the reins. This form is always permissible for general riding but look out if you want

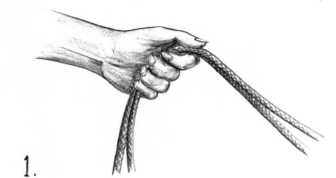

1.

Split reins held in "open hand"

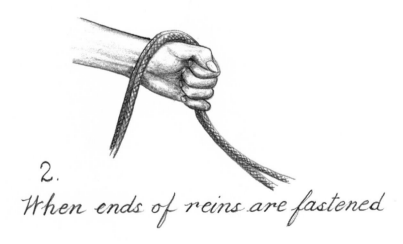

2.

When ends of reins are fastened

to enter a horse show. The rule will vary from one show to another.

Now, "greenhorns," be careful if you want to impress your friends with your riding know-how. There are a few things you must remember. Hanging on to the saddle horn is bad, bad, bad, no matter how inviting it may look. And sometimes it really does! The saddle horn was designed for a purpose; for one thing, it is a solid place to secure a working rope. It is not a security blanket. The average western rider is expected to be able to hold and maintain his balance without any help from the saddle. (You may see riders resting their hands on the horn and leaning slightly toward it, but this is a jaunty pose more than anything else and is done only in informal circumstances. It is a far cry from holding on for dear life.) The saddle horn was not designed for you to sling a leg over either. Every good horseman knows that the saddle was designed for a rider to sit in, straight and tall. The minute you vary from that posture you create "hot spots" on your horse. Hot spots occur when circulation under the saddle is prevented because the rider is leaning heavily on one area, causing extra pressure. Get off if you want to stretch.

The knowledgeable rider pays extra attention to his tack, too. When "saddling up," he always checks his saddle blanket first to see that it is clean of branches, pebbles, or burrs, and he makes sure that it rests smoothly on his horse. He protects his saddle when not in use either by hanging it up or by resting it on something. If it must be laid on the ground, it is placed upright with the horn facing the ground.

A friend called me recently to tell me her exciting news. Her husband had announced that he was treating the family to a two-week vacation at a dude ranch. She was thrilled, of course. "But," she wailed, "what on earth are we going to wear? Our boots and breeches would look ridiculous in a western saddle. What am I going to do?"

Well, if you ever find yourself in that wonderful predicament, remember, western riding attire is just as practical as the horse. You will have to buy a few things, but chances are excellent the money won't be wasted because you'll find opportunities to wear them over and over again when you get back home.

Starting at the top, you'll need a western hat with a wide brim and a high crown. The style worn is whatever style looks best on the rider, so be choosy. You'll find one that's good for you. The practicality of this type of hat is obvious. The wide brim is an excellent sunshade and protector from rain. The high crown allows air to circulate, giving much more comfort to the rider, especially on hot days. The hat should fit snugly with no tie under the chin. Ties can be dangerous. The western hat is a light hat and if it should be knocked off or caught in a branch, the rider stands a good chance of being strangled if the tie doesn't give. Don't laugh; it has happened!

Buy a long-sleeved riding shirt, preferably from a shop selling riding equipment. The shirts there are especially designed to give you freedom in the saddle. Naturally, long-sleeved shirts will give you greater protection when riding through brush. You can always roll up the sleeves if the weather is hot but it's awfully nice to have that protection if you need it. Western styles come and go with changing fashions. Choose the shirt according to today's fashion market, but be selective. It will last much longer. There is such a fine line between blatant attire and tasteful attire. When in doubt, neat conservative styles and muted colors are always acceptable and appropriate.

Most riders wear a well-fitting pair of jeans—well-fitting meaning not so tight that they bind, nor so loose that they rub. There are also some very attractive western riding pants on the market. Take your choice. And ladies, check out the fit of tight pants. Girl-watchers have even gone so far as to number degrees of tightness from one to ten, one being the loosest, ten the tightest. Don't be a number nine or ten! You'll never hear about it, but you sure will be talked about.

The pants are worn long so that when mounted only the shoe of the boot shows.

You may like to buy a pair of chaps (pronounced "shaps"), shotgun

Informal Western Attire
horse equipped with Bosal

chaps, or chinks. They are not necessary but they do provide extra protection to the rider's legs as he travels through underbrush or in the rain and often they help reduce slipping in the saddle. You can wait until you get to your destination to buy them if you like.

Do get a pair of western boots. They are sold in a variety of styles. The heel is higher than the normal shoe in order to keep the foot from slipping forward through the wide stirrup. The height of the boots varies. They should be high enough to keep your feet from getting soaked when walking on muddy ground or through shallow streams. They are also excellent protection against snake bites. Make sure you get boots that fit comfortably when you're walking. You're going to be in them a lot.

Spurs are optional but should be blunt-edged if worn. Sharp, roweled spurs are fancy but not practical, for spurs are used only at selected times, and then with great care, to help the horse, not to injure him. Only the experienced rider has the ability to do this successfully. The average rider (and this means most of us) does not.

Take along a short parka if you think you'll be riding in the mountains. The air gets cold when the sun goes down. Also a slicker to protect you from rain and wind. A hunter's poncho is perfect if you have one among your camping equipment. It folds flat when not in use and yet is large enough to cover all of you and most of the saddle when needed.

The style of saddle you'll be riding in depends upon the type of work each horse and rider will do. The three most popular types are the double-rigged (heavy saddle with two cinches), the three-quarter-rigged (medium-weight saddle with two cinches), and the centerfire (light saddle with only one cinch). Some western saddles are plain leather, some are beautifully and decoratively tooled, and some have trappings of silver and other decorative appointments. Fortunately for our pocketbooks, beauty will never be more important than neatness and utility for the western rider.

The trail rider will more often ride in a full double-rigged saddle because it's comfortable, won't slip and slide going up and down hills, is sturdy, and holds up well in any kind of weather. However, skillful riders

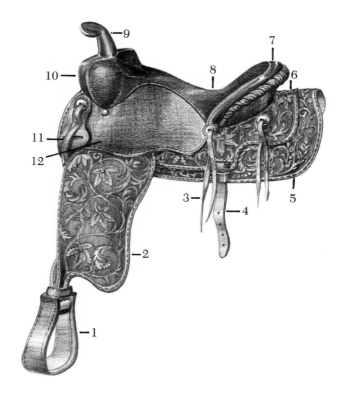

WESTERN SADDLE

1. Stirrup
2. Fender
3. Saddle string
4. Flank billet
5. Skirt
6. Apron
7. Cantle
8. Seat
9. Horn
10. Fork
11. Cinch strap carrier
12. Jockey

may have the opportunity to try their hand at specialized events which include speed. Those riders may need the lighter, less cumbersome saddle.

Every western saddle is worn with a blanket to protect the horse's back from friction and sore spots. Color is permissible and Indian blankets are sturdy and most attractive.

There are several kinds of bridles. The most common, because it is a gentle bridle, is the split-ear bridle used with a grazing bit. The spade bit is most commonly used if the horse's way of going is strong and he needs a more severe bit to be controlled. The western horse rarely needs a noseband for normal riding. But trail riders might put one on if they think they'll be traveling through rough country and need extra security. The noseband is a small strip of leather that lies across the nose and attaches onto the cheek straps. The cavesson-type noseband (a piece of leather that fits entirely around the nose with another strip that runs up and over the head) is used mostly by English riders.

Sometime in your travels you'll meet a bitless bridle called a hackamore adopted from our Spanish forebears. The nose piece on this kind of bridle is called a bosal and works properly when it hits the front of the nose about an inch above the area where cartilage and bone join. Control is maintained through the nose button on the front and the knot under the chin. The word *hackamore* comes from the Spanish word *jaquima*. When riding with a hackamore, the rider's hands must be light. A great deal of pressure is placed on a particularly sensitive area and air is cut off when pressure is applied to the nose button. Special jaquima classes in horse shows are available for those who wish to ride horses with a hackamore.

If there is ever a time when a rider must pay particular attention to his horse and his equipment, it is when riding western style. Remember, western saddles are heavy, even the light ones. Any saddle must be placed gently and carefully upon a horse's back. And, if the saddle is full-rigged (that is, has two cinches instead of one), don't forget the rear cinch. It is there to be used. Draw it up so it is snug but not tight. Often one sees riders with the rear cinch hanging loose. This is dangerous because a horse can

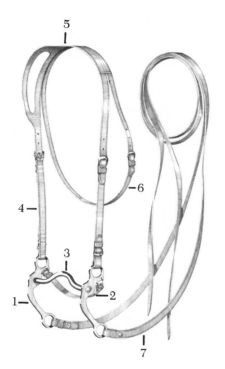

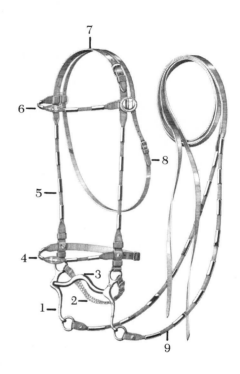

WESTERN BRIDLE (SPLIT-EAR)

1. Grazing bit
2. Curb strap
3. Port
4. Cheek piece
5. Headstall
6. Throatlatch
7. Rein (open)

WESTERN PARADE BRIDLE

1. Cutting horse type bit (loose ring)
2. Curb chain
3. Port
4. Noseband
5. Cheek piece
6. Browband
7. Headstall
8. Throatlatch
9. Rein (open)

catch his foot in the cinch by even so simple a movement as kicking at a fly! In rough country where a horse gathers his legs underneath him and scrambles, the danger is even greater! If you stop for a rest somewhere and loosen your cinches (which you should do), throw the stirrup over the saddle to remind you to tighten them back up again before you go. And when you're ready to take the saddle off, always unbuckle the rear cinch first. The rear cinch is not tight enough to keep the saddle in place if the horse bolts after you undo the front cinch.

Western riding is relaxed, easy, and free. But make no mistake, it is *never* careless.

BASIC HORSE-SHOW ATTIRE AND PRACTICE

Look out, show riders! Since formal western riding is new to the world compared to the more classic English riding, horse-show associations are not all in agreement. Correct riding position and even attire are not the same throughout the country. Expect that rules will vary and make it your business to find out which association and which rules will govern any show you want to enter.

Despite the differences, all of the associations are agreed that the judge should look for a kind disposition, quiet manners, easy gaits, and perhaps good conformation. And all of the organizations have classes designed to show off the western horse in all the phases of work western horses have had to do in the past.

There are class divisions for trail horses, pleasure horses, cutting horses, and roping horses. There are gymkhana events that demonstrate quick turning skill and there are jaquima classes. So take your pick. There are classes to fit every horse and everyone's taste.

Trail classes are designed to show smoothness of gait at the walk, jog trot, and lope and to indicate a horse's good sense when he faces the typical obstacles on the average trail ride. He might, for example, have to cross a bridge, drag firewood, or even carry double. The trail horse must back carefully and he is expected to stand still when mounted from either side. (Try mounting out in the country on the downhill side of a horse sometime. He suddenly becomes ten feet tall!)

Cutting horses are judged for their ability to cut out a calf from a herd and stock-horse classes exhibit agility, speed, quietness, and roping ability. What fun these divisions are to watch! I marvel at the horses' intelligence and sensitivity to the situation at hand. Those horses have learned their job and do it so well.

Gymkhana events include barrel racing and pole bending among others. Needless to say, special events take great training and careful attention must be paid to the horse's conditioning and to proper bitting.

I watched a barrel-racing class not too long ago. One man raced his horse into the ring and then proceeded to make a mockery of the very reason the class was invented—to exhibit his horse's skill. The horse was equipped with a severe bit, and to make matters worse, each time the horse was to bend around a barrel, the rider swung his hands across his horse's neck so hard the horse could defend himself only by throwing his head up in pain. The rider's brute strength got the horse around the course. Then in came another horse with a young boy aboard. The bridle was simple, the rider attuned to his horse. His hands were gentle and his weight shifted to help his horse, not hinder him. As a result, the horse flew around the course with his head down and his ears forward. He could see where he was going!

The American Horse Shows Association rules state that "the western rider's clothing must be clean, neat, and workmanlike." Any type of secure western hat is acceptable, and you should wear a long-sleeved, well-fitting shirt. Don't get too jazzy—this is a working outfit, remember? Chaps are required unless otherwise specified in the show rules. The boots are western type as are the spurs, which are optional, but blunt-edged if used.

A rope is usually carried even if it is not to be used. Because the rope is carried on the right side by right-handed people and on the left side by left-handed people, the rope helps designate to the judge whether the rider is left- or right-handed. In equitation classes the rope is the proof that the rider is holding his reins in the correct hand.

Make sure the saddle fits the rider. Although there is no prerequisite for the type of saddle used, a small rider would look ridiculous in a saddle designed to fit a 200-pound man. He certainly couldn't carry it!

Any standard western bit is acceptable. So are curb chains, but rules state the size allowed. Don't go overboard with severe bitting. Train your horse instead.

Silver on the bridle or saddle is always beautiful and always expensive. If a fancy saddle doesn't fit into your budget, don't worry. No matter how beautiful the other saddles may be, they will never be counted over a good working saddle and bridle.

Bosals, cavesson-type nosebands, hackamores, and tiedowns (a form of martingale) are always prohibited in stock, trail, and pleasure classes unless specifically stated in the show rules. Once again, I repeat! The horse that can perform the best with the least amount of equipment is the horse you want. Proper training is all-important.

Some associations require that you carry hobbles if your reins are attached. No hobbles are necessary if the reins are split. The reason is obvious. Western riders still find it necessary to dismount from their horses in order to carry out their work. Split reins are easy to tie around a tree or a fence, and there is no danger of a horse getting his leg caught in split reins. But if the reins are not split, they remain on the horse's neck and hobbles are used to keep the horse from wandering away. Hobbles should be tied on below the cantle on the near side of the saddle.

Don't be fooled by the easiness and relaxed atmosphere at the show. Western horsemen get just as nervous and they pay just as much attention to their horse and attire as their English counterparts.

Every horse is carefully groomed. His mane and tail are not braided but the mane is thinned and shortened according to the horse's conformation and both are carefully combed.

Although a rider may choose to wear a long, well-fitting pair of western

Hat

String tie

Coat

Shirt

slip-on spur

spur + strap

Pants

Ranch boot with "walking heel"

dip top boot

Men's Formal Western Attire

felt hat

straw hat

Shirt & tie

Scarf

Vest

Coat

Pants

Boots

Ladies Western
Mix or Match Attire for Show or Parade

riding pants and forget the chaps in pleasure classes (chaps may or may not be required depending on the rules of that particular show), there are also extremely attractive full western habits which he may prefer to wear instead. A man always wears a tie when wearing the full habit. (He usually wears one with western riding pants, too.) A word of warning: watch the length of the jacket. It should not bunch at the bottom when you're sitting in the saddle. A woman may wear the full habit but more often she'll wear a long-sleeved shirt with an attractive vest that complements her shirt and legwear. All jackets, vests, and legwear should fit well. When they do not, a rider's appearance is hurt even though he may have excellent skills. I saw a rider lose a horsemanship class because her jacket was large and bulky, and made her look as though she was slumping in her saddle. Even the best judge can be fooled, especially when there are many riders in the ring. Pay special attention to your attire. It *is* important!

11

The English Seat

In the distant past only the upper classes and perhaps an elite military corps were privileged to own and ride horses. Hardly anyone else at that time could afford a horse, much less have one strictly for pleasure. If by some fluke they did have one, it was usually a plow-horse type, not finely bred or capable of moving cross-country with any speed or flair.

Manners! Dress! Elegance! They were a way of life for the upper class. It was only natural that they would retain that same elegance while riding and driving their horses.

In the United States the English style of riding evolved in two directions: hunt seat and saddleseat. As riding technique for each form was developed and refined, the tack and attire changed accordingly. But each seat remains a form of English riding.

THE HUNT-SEAT RIDER

"Darn, Darn, *Darn!*" I watched a young boy sputter as he sailed through the air minus his horse after misjudging a fence. He grumbled loudly as he landed, rose to his knees, took off his hunt cap, and beat it into the

ground. Then, still mumbling to himself, he climbed back aboard his horse to try again.

His riding instructor and I could do nothing but look at each other and laugh. We knew how he felt. We knew, too, how much he had to remember. Where do I put my reins? What is my position in the saddle? How am I and my horse going to meet each fence? How many strides do I take between fences? How fast or slow a pace? Learning to ride a hunter well is no small job. It takes time, training, experience, and, most definitely, a few falls along the way.

Another young woman, a fine western rider, recently moved to a different part of the country and, as hunters were more prevalent in her new area, she decided to try her hand at hunt-seat riding. "I'm *never* going to learn," she wailed one day. Well, I've watched her ride. She's not nearly as bad as she thinks she is (she's a perfectionist at heart). Most of us would be delighted to do as well. But it is true she's not as capable nor does she feel as secure in her English saddle as she did in her western one. I repeat: It takes time. She forgets she is now mounted on a horse trained totally differently from the one she has known all her life. She must work to adapt to her new style of riding.

One major difference between the hunter and his western cousin is the length of stride. The hunter's walk, trot, and canter are all long. The English rider also learns to post to the trot.

Posting is the forward rising motion the rider uses to maintain his seat more comfortably in the saddle. The rising motion also relieves the horse of the rider's weight—for short moments the rider gives his horse's legs a rest. Anatomically each horse trots on the diagonal (left foreleg, right hindleg touch the ground; then right foreleg, left hind). The rider learns to sit in the saddle as one or the other of the front legs touches the ground. If the rider is traveling in a circle, he must learn to sit in the saddle as the horse's outside front leg touches the ground. Posting on the correct diagonal is an important part of English riding.

Don't worry if you're new to the sport. For a while at least, you'll hear

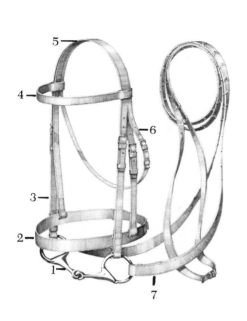

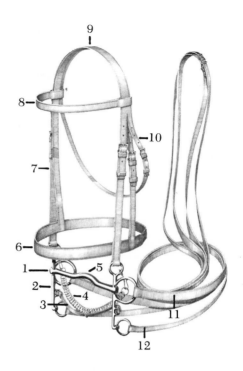

SNAFFLE BRIDLE

1. Egg-butt snaffle bit
2. Cavesson-type noseband
3. Cheek piece
4. Browband
5. Crown piece
6. Throatlatch
7. Snaffle rein (not sewn-in)

PELHAM BRIDLE

1. Pelham bit
2. Cheek piece on pelham bit
3. Lip strap
4. Curb chain
5. Port
6. Cavesson-type noseband
7. Cheek piece
8. Browband
9. Crown piece
10. Throatlatch
11. Snaffle rein (sewn-in)
12. Curb rein (sewn-in)

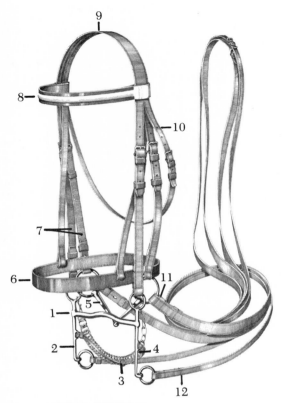

FULL BRIDLE

1. Curb bit
2. Cheek piece on curb bit
3. Lip strap
4. Curb chain
5. Snaffle bit
6. Cavesson-type noseband
7. Cheek pieces
8. Browband (saddle horse type)
9. Crown piece
10. Throatlatch
11. Snaffle rein (not sewn-in)
12. Curb rein (not sewn-in)

your instructor repeating those horrible words "up-down, up-down" in your sleep. But once you gain a little confidence in yourself and begin to feel the actions of your horse beneath you, you will learn to post correctly.

All of a horse's forward motion begins in the hindquarters, so the faster or more pronounced the gait, the more work the hindquarters must do. The canter is simple. The rider sits comfortably, almost erect in the saddle, just as he would when riding a western horse.

Jumping is another matter. The rider has to learn to raise himself up and stay forward out of the saddle not only to maintain his own balance but to relieve his horse from any extra weight he might unconsciously place upon the hindquarters. That position takes practice. Don't expect to learn overnight. It won't happen!

There's a vast assortment of riding equipment to learn about too. Learn the parts of bridles and saddles and you're well on your way to impressing your friends with your horse knowledge. Learn how they work and you're well on your way to becoming a real horseman! Don't be afraid to ask questions.

There are three types of bridles generally used by the hunt-seat rider:

1. The *snaffle,* which is equipped with a gentle bit and one set of fairly wide reins.

2. The *Pelham,* which consists of a more severe bit, a curb chain, a lip strap, and two sets of reins. The snaffle rein is the wider of the two reins. The curb rein is narrow.

3. The *full bridle,* which includes both a snaffle and a curb bit and two sets of reins.

All of the bridles are equipped with a brow band and a cavesson-type noseband. The cavesson is one piece of leather which goes around a horse's nose suspended by another piece of leather which goes up and over the horse's head behind his ears.

The English rider rides with two hands, although many riders prefer to use one hand for relaxed trail riding. Of course you should use one hand

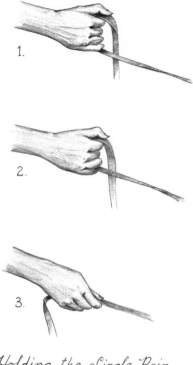

Holding the Single Rein
three ways

only if the horse is well-trained and willing to accept one-handed riding. A rider on a young, inexperienced horse must use two hands. Two hands or one, try not to let your hands wander all over the place, a major fault in English riding. They must remain still, one hand on each side of the horse's neck, thumbs up. Try to think of holding the reins as you would hold a bicycle. The reins are the handlebars and the horse's head the imaginary wheel in between. It will help keep your hands quiet.

There are three correct ways to hold single (snaffle) reins.

1. The rein is held in the palm of the hand, which is in a relaxed position (pretend you are shaking hands), the ends coming out between the thumb and forefinger.

2. The rein is carried between the little finger and ring finger, the ends coming out between the thumb and forefinger.

3. The open hand (very gentle): The rein is held in the entire hand. It runs through the thumb and forefinger, the end coming out behind the little finger. The open hand is not common today but is still used by skillful horsemen when they are riding a horse with an exceptionally sensitive mouth.

Whereas western reins are split, English reins are usually buckled together. The bight of rein (the ends nearest you) may fall on either side of the saddle. However, the reins are always picked up at the buckle and then the rider's hands are adjusted to the reins.

Those riding with double reins hold the snaffle (the wider rein) as described in number 1 above. The curb rein (the narrower rein) goes between the ring finger and the little finger. The ends of both snaffle and curb come out between the thumb and forefinger. It is customary in the United States to hold the curb rein looser than the snaffle. There are some parts of Europe where custom dictates the reins be reversed.

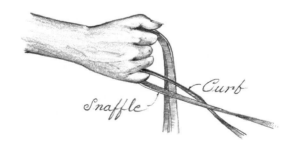

Holding Double Reins

The English saddle, because it is light in comparison to its western counterpart, can be used either with or without a saddle pad. If a saddle pad is used, it is cut to the shape of the saddle and its color is strictly conservative. The saddle is much lighter in weight than the western saddle; the rider wants his horse to be as free as possible when jumping or moving on at a fast pace.

Every rider, as he becomes more skilled, gets more and more particular about the type of saddle he uses. Forewarned is forearmed! Don't let anyone talk you into buying a saddle unless you're sure you'll be comfortable in it. We're all different shapes and sizes. A second-hand bargain for someone else may not be a bargain for you.

It's better to spend a little more money and *know* you'll be comfortable. I have to use a soft, well-padded saddle to protect my back. I'm well aware that it isn't as efficient as a slimmer saddle would be, especially when training green horses, since I can't feel the movements of the horse as easily. But for me it's necessary. Take your time and look around when you're ready to buy a saddle. There are many varieties to choose from, ranging from the very flat saddle used by the dressage rider performing in an enclosed area to the "Periani," an extreme forward seat saddle made by the Italians specifically for comfort in jumping high fences. The saddle may or may not have knee rolls, although knee rolls afford better security for those who wish to jump.

Good leather, carefully sewed, is the other crucial thing to look for. And one last word. Make sure the saddle fits your horse. His comfort is important, too.

Perhaps, Mom and Dad, this situation applies to you. You have a son or daughter who has literally gone berserk over horses. He or she has begged and pleaded for riding lessons and you've finally decided to give in. Besides, if you're like many of the parents I know, you've decided that you might like to try it too. Everyone seems to have so much fun (those Sunday-morning brunches and stirrup cups are right up your alley); you are the athletic sort and "anything my kid can do, I can do," right? Absolutely right! Go to it. Riding is a true family sport and can be enjoyed throughout your lifetime. Do remember, though, the heritage of formality. Your horse, well groomed; your equipment, well kept; and your attire, appropriate for the occasion.

Riders everywhere are gregarious. There are riding clubs that organize "get-togethers" and riding stables and hunt stables that do the same. In every case, formality is expected of their members at one time or another.

The time of day and the occasion help dictate the proper attire. A Saturday-morning ride, for example, calls for more relaxed attire than an invitation to tea after your ride. If you're invited to tea, you're going from your horse to the drawing room. Don't just throw on a pair of dirty boots

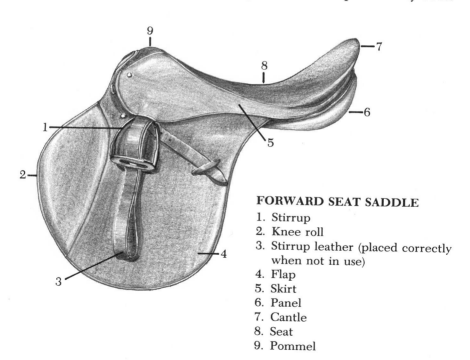

FORWARD SEAT SADDLE
1. Stirrup
2. Knee roll
3. Stirrup leather (placed correctly when not in use)
4. Flap
5. Skirt
6. Panel
7. Cantle
8. Seat
9. Pommel

and jeans. I guarantee no one will say a word to you but the smiles will not be the cordial ones you had hoped to receive and you may not be invited back.

Everyone in the riding world recognizes that riding clothes are expensive. Save your very best attire for social occasions and horse shows. Everyone else is doing the same.

To be practical, many riders wear stretch jeans or other well-fitting long pants and a neat, tailored shirt when schooling. Shoes are a matter of preference. Some people wear high riding boots, either leather or rubber, under their jeans while others wear a sturdy shoe or boot. Sneakers are never worn because they are light and have no heels, and a rider's foot can slip too easily through the stirrup and get caught. Chaps (pronounced "shaps") have been adopted from the West and are a great boon because they give a rider extra security in the saddle and are durable and practical for everyday wear. If you decide to wear chaps, wear them only with informal, relaxed attire—over jeans or other pants, not over the more formal breeches and boots. Wear one or the other, not both.

Sweaters are well fitting, not tight, but never bulky. The sweater should be tucked into the pants if it is very long. Wear a belt with any pair of pants that has loops provided for a belt.

Jodhpurs (the English type worn with a cuff and no flare at the shoe) are acceptable for any informal or daytime situation. The name stems from the area in which the pants were first developed, Jodhpur, India. Jodhpurs are usually worn with short jodhpur boots although growing children often wear their "jods" under high riding boots. (The high boot is a perfect way to hide that bare area over the ankles that suddenly appears in growing children.) English jods are sold in many colors but the hunt-seat rider prefers shades of tan, yellow, or pearl gray. His jodhpur boots are always *brown*. Those who prefer jods and jodhpur boots or the smart-looking short, laced, brown riding boot wear a brown leather strap around the calf of each leg. It prevents the jodhpurs from slipping on the saddle. The boot strap is always the same color as the boot.

Riders who like to hack in the park wear jodhpurs or they may wear breeches with black or brown high boots. Stick to shades of tan, yellow, or gray unless you can afford more than one pair of breeches. They'll be suitable for even the most formal occasion. Brown or rust-colored breeches are really good-looking but only acceptable for informal wear.

The high boots also come in a variety of styles and are available in both leather and rubber. Any type of brown or black boot can be worn informally. Only black boots can be worn with formal attire. Women may, if they choose, wear black patent-leather tops with their formal black jacket. They *must* wear them with "very formal attire." (See "Hunting Attire," p. 128.) Gentlemen wear tan tops with black boots only when wearing scarlet and a top hat. Women, unless they are part of a hunt staff, never wear scarlet and never wear tan tops. (Attire does change for Grand Prix show riding. The U.S. Equestrian Team, for instance, rides in scarlet uniform.)

Take care of your leather boots. They need saddle soaping to keep them clean and to preserve the leather just as much as your tack does. Put boot trees in them when they're not in use. Boots have a tendency to sag at the ankles when they're not protected. Fitted correctly, the boot should completely cover the calf and rise to the bend in the knee. Of course, custom-made boots always look elegant. They fit you! Do try on many styles if you must buy off the shelf. You'll find one make of boot will fit better than another.

Select a shirt that is quiet in color or deep in tone. Naturally, a man wears a tie if the occasion is relatively formal. A woman can have a little fun and buy an assortment of chokers which can either match or contrast in color with the shirt. They are acceptable for all but the most formal riding. Most women wear their chokers with a ratcatcher (collarless) shirt or with a boy's shirt with the collar removed. The ratcatcher shirt is a versatile, attractive, long-sleeved, collarless shirt which comes supplied with a detachable, long, narrow tie. The tie, if it is worn, is tied as a bow tie and is always the same material as the shirt. In riding vernacular, a rider may be requested to wear "ratcatcher" (meaning informal attire).

Don't get carried away in the tack shop. If you're not sure of yourself steer away from the loud riding jackets and buy a tweed. Tweed is always

Hunt cap

Derby

Crop or Bat

Ratcatcher shirt

Shirt & tie

Coat

Jodhpurs

Breeches

Jodhpur boots

Boots

Informal Hunt Seat Attire

beautiful, never goes out of style, and it doesn't show the dirt. The jacket should have a flared skirt and be split at the tails so that it will fit smoothly while you're sitting on a horse. Don't forget to bend your arms to see if the sleeve is long enough. Buy a jacket large enough to wear over a sweater or vest if you like to ride in cold weather. (The really sharp-looking rider wears his sweater and long underwear under his shirt and tie.)

Informal riders, except in the show ring, can choose whether to wear a hard hat or not. Every rider should wear one if he plans to jump. Ladies, this is no time to be vain. Wear a hat, make sure it fits securely and squarely on your head. Worry about your hair later. The hat is there for your safety.

A hunt cap is acceptable for everyone informally. A man may splurge and buy a specially designed hard snap-brim hat in tweed—not very practical at today's prices but if it fits well, it does look marvelous. Many men and women prefer to wear a derby, especially if they're fox hunters. Adults must wear a derby in the hunt field. That is part of the uniform. The derby, too, is hard and designed to protect the head. It has the added attraction of a brim, which comes in handy if the rider is traveling through underbrush as it deflects the twigs that might otherwise scratch his face. The brim does wonders at keeping the rain off the back of the neck, too.

Basic Horse-Show Attire and Practice: The time has come. You've had enough lessons and for many weeks your instructor and your friends have been encouraging you to enter a show. So one day you agree. I know and you know that deep down in your heart you've really wanted to try your hand at showing for a long time. It's just that you're afraid you'll make a fool of yourself. And, in fact, it's only too true that you might. Horses are extremely clever at making fools of all of us at one time or another. On the other hand, you will have fun and show people are wonderful. If you're dressed correctly, know your skills reasonably well, and are mounted on a horse that is capable of doing his job, you'll be applauded and encouraged, win or lose. That's sportsmanship and the very essence of riding.

Show hunters are a breed of horses unto themselves. They are usually finer in appearance than the hunter who actually hunts in the field although there are some horses who can do both. The show rider is demonstrating the smoothness of his horse's way of going, so his horse is often ridden more slowly than he might be ridden in the hunt field.

Today's hunters in the horse-show world are predominantly Thoroughbred or Thoroughbred-type horses. (A Thoroughbred is a particular breed of horse just as is the Morgan, Quarter Horse, and others. The word is not to be confused with "purebred," which can be applied to any true breed of horse.) Thoroughbreds are popular because of their beauty and because of their extraordinary ability to take any kind of fence. Of course English show riders can also be seen upon Quarter Horses, Arabians, and many other breeds of horses too, particularly in pleasure- and trail-horse classes. Any type horse that moves smoothly over fences and who seems comfortable and easy to control will do well in hunter trials and other shows especially designed for the field hunter. So hang on to your Roman-nosed, big-footed horse if he pleases you. There's a place for him in the show world, too. Just don't put him in conformation classes in top-rated shows where he'll be outclassed by his streamlined competitors.

Horse-show attire for the hunt-seat rider seems more complicated than it really is. If you've been taking lessons for a while or have become involved with a social riding group you probably already have most of the equipment you'll need for the average show ring. If you've been wearing jodhpurs and feel comfortable in them, continue to wear them. Put on your brown jodhpur boots, your ratcatcher shirt, a nice tweed jacket, your hunt cap, and go. Women can wear a contrasting choker. Gentlemen (those over eighteen) and boys wear white shirts and a tie in a color complementary to their riding jacket. Young boys look nice in a bow tie. If you prefer to have a riding jacket that is all one color rather than a tweed, go ahead and get one. Just be sure the color is deep, not bright. Navy blue and hunter green are two good choices. A white linen jacket in warm weather is smart-looking and, oh so cool, but it does get dirty quickly. Black jackets can be worn any time in the show ring but they are only worn with a white shirt and a white stock, never with a ratcatcher.

Juniors, that is, everyone under the age of eighteen, must wear a

Hunt Cap

Choker

light-weight Crop or Bat

Safety Harness

Girl's Shirt

Boy's Shirt with tie

Coat

Gloves

Knee Garter

Foot Strap

English Jodhpurs

Laced Riding Shoe or Jodhpur Boot

Child's Attire for English Seat · Show or Field

reinforced hunt cap. Adults dressed informally may wear a cap or a derby. The cap may be either brown, black, or rust. Juniors must wear a black cap when riding in formal attire. Adult men and women, wear a black derby when dressed formally.

Riders who prefer breeches wear them in shades of tan, canary, or pearl gray. Brown or rust breeches are acceptable too, but not for formal riding. The shirt, choker, or tie are in colors complementary to the jacket.

Formal show attire is exactly the same as formal hunting attire. (See "Hunting Attire," p. 128, for the specifics.) Many shows offer appointment classes. The rider's formal attire and his horse's equipment are included in the judging score. In the past the rules for appointment classes were very strict. A woman was expected to carry a sandwich and tea in the sandwich case, which was attached to the saddle. A gentleman carried not only a sandwich in his sandwich case but a separate flask, which had to be filled. Today neither the sandwich case nor the flask need be filled. Junior boys are no longer required to carry the flask. All juniors may continue to wear the black hunt cap even though they are required to wear a derby after age sixteen in the hunt field.

Tack appointments are equally important. Although the bridle may be full, Pelham, or snaffle, all leather must be flat and adults must have sewn-in reins. Juniors are not required to have sewn-in reins. A cavesson noseband must be used. No saddle pad is worn under the saddle. Elastic girths are not acceptable and girth guards must be worn in place over the billets.

Riders must have spurs and hunt whips for appointment classes. The spurs are blunt-edged and the leather straps that hold the spurs on the boot are always the color of the boot and are worn high on the boot. The spur shank points down.

Be careful when purchasing a hunt whip. Some hands are smaller than others. Try out several before you decide to buy. Although both a bat (thick handle) and a crop (thin handle) are carried at the end of the shaft, the whip is held close to the middle of the shaft. The thong stretches the length of the shaft and is then looped loosely about three times. It can be quite a handful. Practice riding with one before you enter an appointment class. It's not uncommon for a rider to poke himself in the eye or lose his reins when he first learns to ride with a whip.

A bat or a crop may be carried at any time other than in appointment classes. If one is carried, it is always carried by the inside hand, "inside" being defined as the inside of the circle, real or imaginary, that the horse travels.

So watch out. Many, many riders have lost their blue ribbon because *something* was wrong with their appointments. A checklist isn't a bad idea at all.

Now that we've got you all settled, don't forget your horse. Whatever the class, he must look as elegant as you. His mane and forelock should be thinned and about five or six inches in length. Snip a small amount of hair from his poll and near his withers to allow the bridle and saddle to fit comfortably. The whiskers on his nose and the hairs in his ears are trimmed to show his beautiful head and the feathers on his legs are trimmed to show off his neat ankles. The tail is not necessarily thinned but sometimes it is shortened so that it drops no farther than his point of hock. It may be blunt cut or it may be carefully cut and thinned to appear more natural. Whichever looks more attractive. The tail is always brushed and combed carefully. Groom him with a curry comb and a brush until he shines.

The mane and usually the tail are braided for major shows. It doesn't matter how many braids the horse has but it is important that they all lie on the same side (usually the off side) and are neatly done. Most people braid with heavy-duty thread in the same color as the mane. Some will braid with a small amount of yarn that complements the color of their riding jacket. I prefer the thread. Most yarns give a heavy look to the mane and neck.

The tail braid starts at the dock of the tail and goes down about nine or ten inches. The rest of the tail is left to flow free. Don't wait until the day of the show to learn how to braid your horse. Believe me, it's not as simple as it looks. Oh, the wails I have heard from instructors who, too late, see their students enter the show ring on horses whose braids are sort of half in and half out. Don't let it happen to you. Good-looking, secure braids are mastered only after much practice.

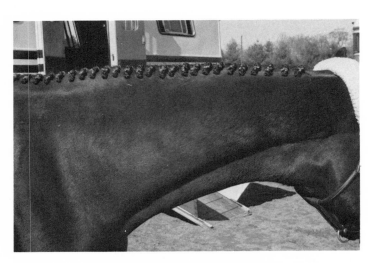

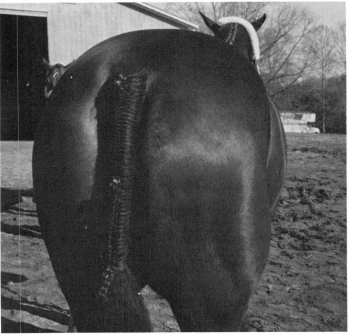

Hunter classes are divided into divisions in the major shows. First-year green hunter classes are designed for hunters in their first year of showing over fences regardless of their age. The jumps are low and the course is simple. Second-year green hunters are expected to perform more ably. The jumps are higher and the course more difficult. Regular hunter classes are designed for the horse with two years or more of showing behind him. He'll jump four-foot fences easily and he's not frightened by the crowds or by the variety of fences.

In working hunter classes horses are judged on performance only. In conformation hunter classes horses are judged on conformation as well as on performance.

A "flat" or under-saddle class is one in which the horse is judged at the walk, trot, canter, and sometimes hand gallop (a controlled gallop). The horse is not expected to jump and is not allowed to wear a martingale. Green horses are not expected to hand gallop.

There are pleasure classes and trail classes too. Most of the time beauty is not a real prerequisite in these classes. A horse's manners and his way of going are of far greater importance.

Horse showing is a way of life for some people. Others show only occasionally. But whichever group you fall into, you'll make friends with people who share your interests, and you'll learn a great deal just from watching.

There are specialized fields of English riding that have grown tremendously in the past few years.

Dressage: Actually, elementary dressage can best be defined as schooling (teaching) the horse to perform his natural gaits to the best of his ability. Formal advanced dressage or Haute Ecole includes all the fine points of English riding done upon a highly schooled horse. The advanced rider and his horse not only learn to perform highly collected movements (as demonstrated by the famous Spanish Riding School in Vienna), but also learn to extend (stretch out) the paces and to move on a free (loose) rein. Horse and rider execute, too, continuous transitions of pace (that is, from fast to slow to fast again and/or from walk to canter to trot, etc.). Repeated changes of lead within short intervals are also done; it almost looks as though the horse were skipping.

There are many dressage levels of competition so even the novice rider and his novice horse are encouraged to participate, learn, and have fun. The advanced levels of dressage are difficult, to say the least, to execute correctly. It takes years of training, as does any art, and it is always supremely beautiful to watch.

Open Jumping and Grand Prix Jumping: Open jumping is a special division designed to show the horse's ability to take combinations of broad and/or high jumps. How the horse approaches the jump does not matter. The judge is no longer looking for quiet and even pace. However the horse must follow a definite line of course and points are taken off for refusals, knockdowns, deviation of course, and, sometimes, touching the obstacle. The rules are strict in this division and must be adhered to exactly. Time may also be a factor in some open-jumping classes.

Grand Prix jumping is stadium open jumping done on an elegant course designed to show the skill and daring of a horse meeting and going over the very highest and broadest combinations of jumps imaginable. The jumps themselves are decorated with flowers and are extremely colorful. The rider may wear formal hunting attire, his nation's uniform if he is qualified to do so, or white breeches and a scarlet coat. Grand Prix jumping is the only division in which a rider may wear a scarlet coat unless the rider is a master of a hunt or otherwise qualified by a hunt to wear one.

These classes are also supremely beautiful and exciting to watch and require highly skilled teamwork between horse and rider. The U.S. Equestrian Team competes in stadium jumping on an international level.

Combined Training or Three-Day Event: The horse who competes in combined training must be an exceptionally well-rounded athlete. He is expected to travel cross-country over a series of obstacles; he must perform in the dressage ring; and he must be capable of successfully completing a stadium jump course. Points are given for all three phases of the event and the horse with the overall highest score is proclaimed the winner.

There are many different levels of combined training. They range from the lowest level in which any interested rider can participate and have fun to the highest level in which the U.S. team participates. As with any form of riding, the higher the level, the more skill and knowledge required.

THE SADDLESEAT RIDER

"How do I *stop* him?" my hunt-seat husband cried one November day a few years ago. He was mounted upon a Tennessee Walking Horse and the aids he had learned to halt a horse just weren't working. The more he sat back and resisted with his reins, the faster the horse seemed to move. And yet, he discovered later, if he leaned forward a bit and released his reins, the horse would stop. How come? What's with these gaited horses?

Today most saddleseat riders are seen riding horses with exceptionally high front action. Because all the power comes from the horse's hindquarters, riders learn to direct their weight back in the saddle to encourage impulsion (strong, forward movement) and to allow the horse to lift his front legs as high as possible. The American Saddlebred is the horse most generally used although there are those who prefer the Morgan and the Tennessee Walker. These horses, too, have developed high action gaits and saddleseat attire is worn when riding them.

The American saddle horse is truly an American horse. He appeared first in Kentucky and Tennessee during early Colonial times. Horse owners noticed that their common mares bred to the Thoroughbred, Denmark, had foals which developed stylish high-stepping front action to an exceptional degree. To top it off, the foals grew to be as well-behaved for driving as they were comfortable for riding. Either way, the horse had *style!* Horse owners also discovered that wise and prudent breeding developed the saddle horse's way of going even more. And, to top it off, the horse seemed to have a natural talent for two gaits other than the

normal walk, trot, and canter. Thus two "man-made" high-stepping gaits (the slow gait—a four-beat gait done with slight hesitation—and the rack —a speed gait done with precision and exhilaration) came into being. Some horses had more talent than others, so only the best were chosen to learn the slow gait and rack. Experimentation also proved that a longer-than-normal foot shod with a heavier-than-average shoe encouraged the saddle horse to pick up his front feet even more. Unfortunately, many horses' legs were ruined (as they still are today) because unthinking owners immediately tried to shoe *all* their horses with heavy weights regardless of their horse's talents. To make matters worse, they did not slowly and carefully *prepare* and *train* even the talented horses to carry the extra weight. They just threw them on and off they went. The conscientious owner and his farrier pay particular attention to the horse's feet and legs.

They see to it that the horse is not overworked (sometimes working him only fifteen minutes a day) and that he is given a period of time when the weights and the long shoe are removed so he can rest.

Saddleseat riders take care to ride only on well-groomed paths while their horses' feet are long and unnaturally set because balance is extremely difficult for these horses on uneven and rough ground. Pleasure riders keep their horses' feet pretty much at the length most of us are accustomed to seeing. Then the action is not quite so accentuated but the horse is capable of traveling anywhere his master wishes.

At the same time the saddle horse was developed, other owners found that specialized breeding could develop horses with other gaits. The standardbred became a superb pacer and the Tennessee Walking Horse learned the running walk. Some breeds of Morgan were refined and although he maintains only the normal three gaits, the Morgan has that wonderful animated action which attracts the saddleseat rider and driver today.

Saddleseat riding is an offshoot of English riding and therefore the same kind of equipment is used. Most horses are ridden with double reins, although the particular type of bit may vary depending on the amount of control the horse needs. The full bridle or the Pelham bridle (see p. 71) are most commonly used. The Tennessee Walker uses his own specially designed walking horse bit and only one set of reins.

Double reins are not difficult to hold or nearly as complicated as they look. Hold them exactly as you would if you were riding hunt seat or dressage. The little finger is the divider between the two reins. The snaffle rein is the wider of the two, the curb rein the narrower. The curb is more severe because it is attached to the part of the bit that applies the most pressure. The curb rein rests on the inside of the little finger, the snaffle rein on the outside. The hand is held in a relaxed position, palms down but at a slight angle so that the two thumbs form a natural "V." The wrists have a slight downward curve, just enough to prevent them from being rigid.

The body torso and the legs are held in the basic riding position.

Okay, so you're a hunt-seat rider and proud of the way you ride. Now suddenly you're in "gaited-horse" country and there are people doing all

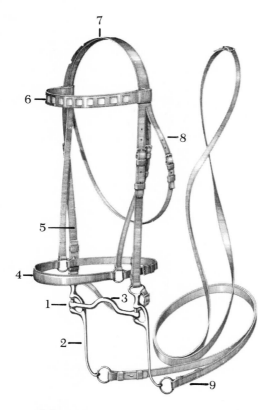

WALKING HORSE BRIDLE

1. Walking horse bit
2. Long cheek piece on bit
3. Port
4. Noseband
5. Cheek piece
6. Browband
7. Crown piece
8. Throatlatch
9. Rein

sorts of things you were taught *never* to do. Don't shake your head and feel superior. It may *appear* to the uninformed that the saddleseat rider is holding his hands abnormally high or that he is sitting too far back in the saddle and, indeed, many are. They are common faults. We all strive for perfection but too few of us achieve it. However, many riders are riding correctly. Just think for a minute. Watch the horse move. The saddle-type horse has a tendency to carry his head much higher than other types of horses, especially hunters. In order to achieve proper contact with his horse the rider must hold his hands high. Similarly, the extreme front action of the horse tends to throw the rider back in the saddle. There is a fine line between those who sit back in order to maintain balance and keep weight off their horse's forequarters and those who *are* sitting too far back. One must look carefully at both the position of the rider and the action and movement of the horse to ascertain whether the rider is sitting correctly in his saddle.

Don't be too quick to criticize. You may be wrong!

The saddleseat rider wears a habit that began as his horse did—in the South. Gentlemen in those times needed riding attire that was appropriate not only for riding but for the drawing room. Often there was no opportunity to change clothes. Thus Kentucky jodhpurs came into being. They are very similar to the jodhpur worn by the English rider but the Kentuckians refined and restyled the "jods" themselves. The pantleg became even more tailored and slim and the cuff was eliminated entirely. A long, slender jacket with a flare in the skirt was adopted at the same time. The jacket was always the same color as the pants and naturally a tie was worn. And no gentleman would appear in public without a pair of gloves. *Style,* ladies and gentlemen, *style!*

Saddleseat attire remains almost the same today for both men and women although informal attire is now most acceptable and far more practical for schooling and exercising. Jodhpur boots or sturdy leather shoes are always worn and a pair of long, slim, but not binding stretch jeans are frequently seen. A neat shirt completes the picture.

As the day progresses and the occasion is social, the attire becomes more formal. A group meeting for an afternoon ride will probably prefer to wear Kentucky jods, jodhpur boots, a neat, soft shirt (not too blatant a color), and of course a sweater if the weather demands. However, on a Sunday, the rider may prefer to dress up. He may appear in the full saddleseat habit: a jacket and jodhpurs of matching material and color. There is a color choice but the most acceptable shades are variations of brown, blue, and deep gray. Black is worn and although acceptable, it does seem a shame to wear such somber attire when riding a horse presenting such a gay appearance.

Saddleseat riders pay particular attention to the fit of their attire. So if you're out to buy yourself a habit, remember that the jodhpurs must be long enough to cover the major part of the boot while you are sitting in the saddle. Don't be deceived by length when you are standing. Go sit down somewhere. Remember, too, that your arms will be bent when aboard your horse. When standing, the sleeve of the coat should reach almost to the tips of the fingers. The jacket sleeve should not bind when your arms are bent and the tips of the sleeves should reach your wrists. No one wants to look as if he's outgrown his attire.

Basic Horse-Show Attire and Practice: "There he goes," shouts a spectator as his favorite horse enters the show ring. A Rebel yell sings out from somewhere in the stands. The whistles begin and so does the laughter. Saddleseat riding is showmanship from beginning to end. None of this conservative-hunter stuff for them. They're out there in the ring to *ride* and show everyone what their horses can *do!* But even with all the cheering and the fun, make no mistake, there *is* a set of rules, and pride in tradition is very evident. Both horse and rider are dressed to the nth degree.

Daytime attire is conservative. The color of the habit is chosen to enhance the color of the horse, not to contrast with him. Shades of brown, blue, gray, and green are favorites. Frills, even on saddle horses, are ridiculous for daytime wear; don't wear them. Bright colors and brocades are not encouraged although they are occasionally worn in the evening. Shiny, glimmery materials are not good for anyone for the simple reason that they draw attention away from the horse. Let's face it. Unless a rider is riding in an equitation class he is supposed to be presenting his horse, not himself. And equitation riders *must* be conservatively dressed.

The habit is worn with a soft, white shirt and the tie is a color complementary to the habit. Light leather gloves are worn by all but the Tennessee Walking Horse rider, who needn't wear them if he prefers not to. The same applies to the hat. Women and children riding walkers are not required to wear a hat when they show, but all other saddleseat riders must. If the hat is required, it should be tight-fitting and set squarely upon the head, not pushed back or off at a jaunty angle. I know the derby is not

Saddle Derby

Shirt

Suit ~ Coat &
Kentucky "Jods"

Gloves

whip

Jodhpur boots

Ladies'
Saddle Seat
Daytime wear for Show or Park

always flattering but as part of the overall appearance, it really looks very smart. Children up to the age of eighteen are required to wear a hard derby for protection. Women may wear either a hard or a soft derby although a hard derby is preferable. The hat is the color of the habit. Gentlemen, even those with walkers, wear a derby or they may choose to wear a snap-brim hat: straw in summer, felt in winter. The snap-brim is preferred by most riders. Women who choose to ride without a hat must pay particular attention to their hair. It should be carefully curled or pinned back and fastened in place.

Style is ever-present. Even the jodhpur strap should be dyed to match the color of the boot.

Spurs and whips are optional. The spurs, if worn, should be secure and placed high on the boot. The rowel should be blunt-edged and should face downward if curved. The whip is finely made, about two and one-half feet long, with a black handle and a white shank. It is always carried by the hand on the inside of the ring and sides should be switched when the rider and horse change direction.

Formal evening attire is impressive. A tuxedo-type one-button saddle suit in either black or midnight blue is appropriate for both men and women and is in excellent taste. The jacket has satin lapels and a satin stripe down the side of the pantleg. The suit is complemented by a cummerbund, a bow tie, and a top hat. The boots may be black patent leather. Again, the straps must match the color of the boot. A boutonniere, either live or artificial, is worn in the evening, never in the daytime. Formal wear has recently become much more fanciful and colorful and this change has carried over into the show ring. Nowadays the shirt may have frills and the jacket may be white or a color. As styles change, so will attire. Let your own good taste prevail. Gaudiness is never acceptable. When in doubt, always stay on the conservative side.

Formal riding habits are *never* worn before 6:00 P.M.

What about the horse? How is he dressed for a show? Well, he's a lot of work.

The tail and the mane are considered a horse's crowning glory, and

Saddle Seat ~ Formal evening wear

great care is taken to develop and accentuate them. One of the ways riders accentuate the tail is to cut the depressor tendons and keep the tail in a special tail set when the horse is not in the show ring. It is believed the practice began because of man's admiration for the horse loose in pasture who arched his tail when he felt playful and full of good spirits. By cutting the tendons, owners found they could keep that same effect at all times. Of course any horse with his tail in a set is carefully watched. He is washed daily and protective devices are placed in the stall to keep him from rubbing his tail against the wall. Many conscientious owners remove the set once the show season is over and let the tail relax until the next show season begins. No horse should be turned out to pasture with his tail in a tail set.

There are some occasions when the mane and tail are not so important. Three-gaited American Saddlebred horses (often affectionately called "walk-trot" horses, although they most definitely do canter) are shown with a roached (clipped) mane and the tail is clipped from the beginning of the tail to approximately halfway down the tail root. The rest of the hair on the tail is allowed to fall free.

The five-gaited American Saddlebred (generally called "gaited" as opposed to his "walk-trot" brother), the Tennessee Walker, and the Morgan (when he is shown in saddle horse classes) are shown with a full mane and tail except for about six inches of mane starting from the poll of the neck, where the mane is clipped to make the horse more comfortable when wearing his bridle. Usually the forelock and one section of mane are braided, for then the head is shown to better advantage.

Some horses, even with the greatest care, don't develop the fullness of mane and tail that is required of show horses. Then (if show rules allow —better check) a portion of artificial tail or switch is carefully added to achieve the desired fullness. The paddock area of the show ring begins to look like a beauty salon. Each horse has his own hairdresser who works and works to achieve his idea of perfection.

Gaited horses, Walkers, and Morgans have their manes braided for show, the purpose again being to show off a fine head. The forelock and the first section of hair in the mane (about 3 inches wide) is braided with satin ribbon (about ⅝ inch wide). The color is optional although many riders select red and white or adopt their stable colors. In any case, the ribbon should not be so loud that it clashes with the color of the horse or his brow band. Colors that suggest something other than horses in a horse show are frowned upon, too—for instance red and green, which denote Christmas, or red, white, and blue, which denote the Fourth of July. The forelock is tucked under the brow band and the top of the cheek piece after braiding to keep it securely in place.

White areas, no matter how pretty, mean *work* for all stable personnel. But no cheating allowed! Using bleaches, dyes, and other devices to enhance the markings or to form markings where there are none is discouraged and even forbidden in some classes.

Because the classes are so exhilarating and gay, many riders get carried away with enthusiasm and attire themselves and their horse a little too blatantly. Be careful. Gaudy attire, tack, or coloring in any class certainly attracts a judge's attention, but often his reaction is the opposite of what the rider intended. There is one standing rule. If a horse is good enough to show, he is good enough to stand on his own four feet. Let him do it! Don't let either of you appear ridiculous. Nothing can beat carefully tailored attire and a horse who knows how to perform.

All tack is made of good-quality leather and is worn with very few frills. There are specific regulations for the type of bridle used, so pay particular attention to the rules set forth in the prize list and bridle your horse according to the rules of the classes you wish to enter. The American Horse Shows Association rule book is an excellent reference. The American Saddle Horse Association, the Tennessee Walking Horse Breeders Association, and the Morgan Horse Association will advise you also.

The only color on the bridle is on the brow band and sometimes the noseband, which are usually made of plastic or patent leather and are well protected when not in use to prevent cracking. Again, color is the rider's choice. As with the braid in the mane, many horses wear their stable colors while other riders choose a color they believe may be more flattering to their horse and to their own riding habit.

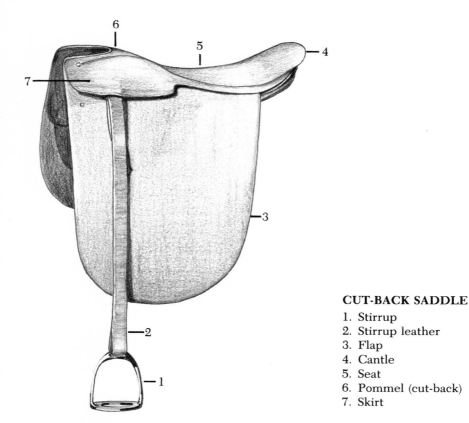

CUT-BACK SADDLE

1. Stirrup
2. Stirrup leather
3. Flap
4. Cantle
5. Seat
6. Pommel (cut-back)
7. Skirt

The saddle is flat and the pommel is cut back. Most saddle-type horses carry their heads high and have short backs. The withers are prominent. The cut-back saddle ensures much greater comfort for the horse because the withers are left free. The illusion of a longer neck is achieved too. The flat saddle is necessary because specialized gaits are more easily performed by horse and rider when the rider's legs are as close to the sides of the horse as possible. Then contact is more constant.

The girth may be plain leather or white web. If white is used, it must be meticulously clean. No saddle pad is used.

Show rules allow boots in some classes, and the rules specify which type of boot may be worn and the weight permitted. Boots are worn on the horse's ankles to prevent cuts and bruises, when, for example, the saddle horse while racking or the Tennessee Walking Horse while performing the running walk tend to become excited and overreach. In other words, the front of the back feet scrape the backs of the front feet. If you've ever been run into by a grocery cart you'll know what I'm talking about. Particular attention must be paid to proper fitting because too tight a boot stops circulation and causes chafing while too loose a boot causes irritation and can interfere with smoothness of gait. Boots are naturally kept as clean as all other equipment.

Combination classes (classes where horses are not only ridden but driven) are offered in some shows. It takes great skill to drive a horse, especially in as small an area as a show ring. And when the horse performs his maneuvers with both animation and flair . . . well, it's something to see. By all means, anyone who has an opportunity to drive should try it. Show rules specify the type of harness and carriage that may be used. The saddle horse is driven in a snaffle bit and pulls a four-wheeled viceroy, which is carefully decorated in the stable colors. Then the harness is removed, the saddle is put on, and the horse is ridden in his regular double bridle.

In every case the judge is looking for the happy, alert horse. He likes to see a horse's ears up and forward, for that is an excellent indication that the horse is happy with his work. And that is why exhibitors encourage spectators to cheer as their horses perform speed gaits. The horse becomes even more animated and seems to catch the enthusiasm of the crowd.

Horse-show observers should not be deceived when watching any horse performing speed gaits. Although the judge is certainly looking for speed, he is looking even more for controlled action. If the horse can be animated and fluid in his motion while maintaining speed, so much the better. But if the judge must choose between two horses—one going very fast but lacking rhythm and the other going slower but more in stride, the ribbon will go to the slower horse. The horse-show ring (except for gymkhana events) is not a race course.

12

Horse Shows

Horse-show people have learned to be prepared for anything and every-thing because anything and everything has happened. The pace of every show alternates between hustling and bustling and slow as the proverbial snail. Nerves begin to show as they always do when one performs and tempers grow shorter as the day goes on. Add to that the fact that horses have a way of getting dirty at the most inconvenient times and pants have a way of splitting just before an appointment class. Children bursting into unexpected tears and loving parents falling apart are not uncommon either. To top it all off, count on the weather at an outdoor show to be temperamental. Hot, hot sun causing sun stroke, windstorms blowing down tents and stabling facilities, hail, sleet, teeming rain, and fog. You name it. It's happened! Yet, despite everything, our horses continue to put up with us and we put up with the turmoil. That's what horse shows are all about. They've been around almost as long as people have had horses, for every horse owner takes pride in his animal and believes his to be the best. Sooner or later he'll want to prove it.

Have you ever thought about the weeks and months of training a rider and his horse must go through in order to spend fifteen minutes in the show ring? Hunters performing on a jump course rarely spend more than two minutes to complete the course. Can you imagine? Months and months of work for two minutes in the show ring! The time, energy, and expense are huge. But it's all worth it, especially when it's your horse that comes out of the ring with the blue ribbon.

Horse-show organizations were formed because rules were needed to ensure a better sense of order to the show world. The Fédération Equestre Internationale (FEI), a body governed by the most respected and able horsemen in the world, is now the final authority over most international events. Almost every nation interested in equestrian activities belongs to the FEI. In turn, each country has organizations that govern different forms of show riding. The American Horse Shows Association is the most widely known in the United States and many of our major shows today are held under its auspices. The American Quarter Horse Association also enjoys great prominence.

It would be foolish for me to put down all of the rules and regulations under which every division of horse (whether it be hunter, Quarter Horse, or whatever) should be shown. Each association selects experienced people from their own field of riding to devise sensible rules and to ensure that their shows are governed as fairly and as humanely as possible. Those who want to know more should contact the American Horse Shows Association, 527 Madison Avenue, New York, N.Y. 10022. For a limited amount of money, the AHSA provides a rule book and a listing of names and addresses of qualified judges and stewards throughout the United States.

Today, horse shows range in size from the small, relaxed country show to the businesslike, highly competitive horse show. Major horse shows are rated A, B, and C. The "A" division show usually has the top-rated horses and riders from all parts of the country. If you and/or your horse are beginners, look first for the C-rated or the nonrated show to allow both of you time to learn and gain confidence and experience. Don't be afraid to make mistakes. We all do. You'll be nervous and so will your horse. Just keep trying. Time will take care of many of your problems.

Schooling shows are unrecognized shows designed specifically to help horse and rider gain experience. They're available almost everywhere at any time of the year and are invaluable to anyone who plans to participate in serious horse showing. They are also great fun for the novice.

Horse shows are designed mostly to exhibit the skill and/or beauty of the horse. Some shows include equitation classes, too, which judge the rider alone on his riding skills, the clothes he wears, and the manner in which he carries himself in the show ring. Conservative riding attire is mandatory, for nothing should detract from the rider showing his skill. Equitation demands are varied depending upon the type of horse one rides and the rules under which each show is governed. The rules are available. Make use of them. The library will have a listing of most national riding and horse associations. Write to the national organization involved with either the type of riding you prefer (such as hunting, jumping, etc.) or the type of horse (such as Morgan, palomino, etc.). Ask for a listing of associations located in your area. Local horse shows usually have names, addresses, and often enrollment blanks, too. Don't be afraid to go to the secretary's desk to ask for information. He or she will be glad to help you. You'll find there are not only national organizations, but state organizations, tri-state organizations, local saddle clubs, and others.

If you have the opportunity to work on a show committee, do so. Don't wait until you are asked. Volunteer to help. In most cases you'll be more than welcome. It's quite an eye-opener to work behind the scenes at a horse show. You'll learn that even the smallest show takes careful planning and a great deal of work. First the committee decides the rules and/or the association under which the show will be given. Then they form a prize list (an advance program), which states: (1) the classes the show will offer; (2) the entry fee for each class; (3) the horse and rider requirements of each class; (4) the date entry fees are due to the show secretary; and (5) all other information the committee deems necessary for the exhibitor to know before he enters the show. The prize list is the source of many groans of despair from committee members before it is ready to be published.

"What have we left out?" is a constant question. "Read it again" is the constant plea.

The committee must find a person or persons competent to judge their show and engage him early. Good judges are in great demand. Wait too long and you won't get one at all. A ringmaster to assist the judge while he is in the ring and a steward or technical delegate to see that the rules of the show are carried out carefully and correctly must also be found.

An injured rider is always an unfortunate possibility although no one likes to admit it. Every committee should arrange to supply an ambulance or have emergency service nearby. A veterinarian and a farrier either at the show or on call are a definite advantage, too. Our Quarter Horse Sam has always been the one of our three horses to get into trouble. One Fourth of July weekend we no sooner arrived at a horse show and backed him out of the trailer than he stepped on a rusty piece of wire that went straight up into his foot. No vet was available or on call at the show. As a result, we had infection and a real mess on our hands by the time a vet could be located many hours later. Help your exhibitors. It will help your show.

A paddock master is assigned to the practice area just outside of the show-ring gate to see that all horses enter the ring when they are called and that classes run as smoothly and as quickly as possible. An announcer is helpful because he can tie the show together by giving instructions to the riders, explaining the instructions to the spectators, and assisting the paddock master whenever necessary by calling horses to the ring, and so on. The announcer in a small show doesn't necessarily need a microphone but a bull horn would certainly help.

A ring crew is enlisted in advance to place and set up jumps, barrels, mailboxes, or any other special equipment needed in each class. There is a tremendous lag in show time if the committee has to hustle up help at the last minute.

Every member of the committee from the chairman to the secretary to the ring crew should be neatly dressed. It gives a uniformity and dignity to the show. If you're a member of the committee, you'll have to stay to the very end. Go prepared for any kind of weather! Raincoats, boots, umbrellas, shade hats, and sweaters—they'll all help at one time or another. You never know what you might need. Plan on a long and hectic day.

The exhibitors for their part should respect the show committee and see that they and their horses are attired correctly and neatly for every class in which they are entered. There is no excuse for anything less. Especially for those who want to show their horses to their best advantage.

The first thing an exhibitor must do after arriving on the show ground is to visit the show secretary and get his number. Every exhibitor wears a special number on his back, which is assigned by the show committee to facilitate horse identification for the judge. Why numbers? Because numbers are far easier to remember and record quickly than many unfamiliar names. If the committee has the opportunity, they'll make up a program for the benefit of the exhibitors and spectators that states the order of the classes and the identification of horse, rider, and number. The program may be as simple as a mimeographed sheet of paper. The main thing is that the information is there.

Good sportsmanship is mandatory. I know it's difficult when nerves are short but bad tempers must be held in control. It's a well-known fact that horses and bad-tempered people are never a good combination. Horses never understand angry punishment anyway and most times the faults of the horse are caused by the faults of the rider. It takes a cool rider to ride an unruly, misbehaving horse well.

Grumbling or loud-mouthing a judge's decision is unacceptable and makes the people who hear it extremely uncomfortable. Be fair. If you have a complaint, report it to the steward. He or she is the person responsible for seeing that show rules are followed. A "difference of opinion" is not a justifiable complaint. We who are watching the show are usually biased. We cannot help but watch our favorites more than we watch our favorite's competitors. Judges, on the other hand, have to watch everyone and try to be as fair and impartial as possible. *Every exhibitor must accept his losses with his wins.*

The exhibitor has several other responsibilities to the show in which he is entered. Each exhibitor should have read the prize list carefully and should fully understand the requirements of each class. He must know that under ordinary circumstances he and his horse can fulfill them successfully. No rider should enter any show ring unless he is confident that he can compete on the same level with every other horse entered. If you aren't sure, don't ask your friends. They may be afraid to hurt your feelings. Ask your local professional. He'll tell you the truth. Riders who enter shows where they are outclassed make terrible spectacles of themselves. Even under ordinary circumstances we all find ourselves in embarrassing situations. What a shame to go looking for them!

Pay attention to the class order and be ready and waiting when it's time for your class to begin. Latecomers are one excellent reason why paddock masters are tearing out their hair by the end of the day. They have enough to do without searching the show grounds for those who are late. Exhibitors should allow themselves sufficient time to warm up their horses before class time, too. The announcer and paddock master will give a first and second warning before each class begins, which should give all riders ample time to arrive in the paddock area. It's a frustration to everyone concerned when a show is held up while a selfish exhibitor takes one last canter or one last jump in the practice area before entering the ring. Remember, if a horse is not prepared before show time, he's not going to be any more prepared by taking that extra jump.

Secure an "order of go" from the paddock master just before the start of your class if you're to perform individually in the ring or over a jump course. Don't wait for him to assign you a number. Go ask for one. Good sportsmanship is imperative at this time, for difficult though it may be, *someone must go first.* The paddock master will try to arrange the order so that each exhibitor need go first only once during the day. Riders, in turn, should inform the paddock master immediately if they plan to ride more than one horse. The paddock master will then try to allow each rider time to change his horse, number, and saddle and to warm up his second horse before going back into the ring. The class moves along smoothly when everyone cooperates.

Your horse should be meticulously brushed and combed and white areas should be well scrubbed. His feet should glisten with hoof polish. Help your horse by applying a small amount of fly spray to protect him if flies are prevalent. Trim the whiskers on the muzzle and the hairs in his ears and around his ankles to give his head and legs an even finer appearance.

Showmanship is very important. Naturally every exhibitor in the ring wants to show off his horse and gain the judge's attention. But showmanship does not include brushing a rider into the rail as one passes, or cutting off another horse from the track in which he is moving. It takes great skill and concentration on the part of a rider to show his horse well but fairly.

Sometimes even the best of riders can be mounted on a horse having what is called in polite terms "a bad day." What happens? Who really knows? The rider's usually quiet, well-mannered mount suddenly sulks, or even worse, kicks, bucks, or, in jumping classes, refuses his fences. Most show committees are grateful to the exhibitor who, when he finds himself in that unfortunate predicament, excuses himself and withdraws from the ring and the competition. There is no rule in any book requesting a rider to do this, but the rider will be respected far more if he excuses himself promptly than if he remains to cause excitement among all the other horses or holds up a jumping class that probably won't count him among the winners anyway. You needn't necessarily excuse yourself if you're in a schooling show, but in rated shows you really should withdraw if you're having this kind of trouble.

We riders can have "bad days" too. Our timing is off. We just can't get together with our horses. I suppose the worst that can happen is that we land on the ground in front of God and everybody. I'm still here and so are many others, which only goes to prove that we do survive.

Each show has its own personality and charm. Some shows are relaxed and informal. At others, there is a great deal of pomp and circumstance. Most shows give at least four ribbons in each class and specify that four horses are necessary to fill a class:

Blue ribbon	1st place	Pink ribbon	5th place
Red ribbon	2nd place	Green ribbon	6th place
Yellow ribbon	3rd place	Purple ribbon	7th place
White ribbon	4th place	Brown ribbon	8th place

Don't be upset if show rules designate that each rider salute an honored guest or judge when entering the ring. It's quite beautiful and not nearly as difficult as it seems. The male exhibitor rides to the honored guest and salutes by removing his hat and then bowing his head, hat and arm at his side. A woman doesn't remove her hat but bows her head briefly, her right hand straight down at her side. Bow your head long enough to count to three slowly. It may seem like forever but, I promise you, it's not.

Horses are called back into the ring in the order in which they are to be presented their ribbons. Don't get so excited about being called back that you forget the order in which your horse was called. Many times the horses are jogged to see that they are serviceably sound—that is, show no lameness. A horse may be excused or he may be dropped a place if he does show signs of lameness. Horses may also be shifted up or down the line in conformation classes where their beauty is part of the total score.

A man removes his hat and nods his head when receiving a ribbon. Sometimes he will place his cap under his left arm and shake hands with the person presenting the ribbons. A woman bows her head briefly. At no time should a rider show disrespect to the judge or to the show committee when he is in the ring. He should remain alert and in good form until he leaves the exit gate. It annoys me to see riders suddenly slump or throw a leg carelessly over the saddle before leaving the ring. To me, that rider doesn't deserve to be there in the first place. Good manners are as much a part of horse showing as expertise in the saddle.

Ribbon hunters are the bane of any small show. Fine horses and skilled riders with lots of show-ring experience shouldn't compete in shows where it is well known that the other horses and riders do not have equal experience and/or ability. There is no show rule to prevent this sort of thing from happening either but the practice is not fair and is certainly morally wrong. It is the responsibility of every person in the horse world to maintain a sense of fair play. It's an unspoken rule and a part of the heritage in which the real horseman takes great pride.

Don't forget, spectators, that you have a responsibility to the show, too. Stay out of the paddock area not only for your own safety but to help the exhibitors. This means you too, mom and dad, unless you're really there to help. The paddock is crowded with many, many nervous horses and riders waiting their turn to enter the show ring. There is rarely room for all the horses to warm up sufficiently. The rider's job is made more difficult when he cannot concentrate on this task but instead must concentrate upon dodging the people on foot.

Show committees have another large gripe: *dogs!* A dog's natural inclination is to chase a moving horse and all kinds of problems result. At the least, a horse and rider's concentration and timing may be lost. Much worse, many horses are afraid of unfamiliar dogs and try to run away from them. Terrible, terrible accidents have occurred. Besides, dog fights are always a possibility and loose dogs love to raid and spill trash cans. They like to run gleefully through spectator areas knocking people over, too. Don't be an inconsiderate spectator. I know you love your dog and want him with you but don't bring him to a show unless you are willing to keep him on a leash with you at all times. Please.

In conclusion, let me stress the fact that entrants in any show must pay particular attention to the prize list and the rules governing the classes they wish to enter. *The rules do vary according to association.* Do not assume anything and never fail to ask questions when you're in doubt. Far better to find out before you enter the show ring what is expected of you and your horse than to be excused or needlessly embarrassed because you were negligent.

13

Fox Hunting

Now suppose that you've been invited to go fox hunting. The "Season" is soon to begin and it's thrilling to know you'll be a part of that magnificent scene you've seen so many times in the movies or in the hunting prints hanging on friends' walls. There's only one problem. You don't know too much about hunting. You feel quite confident about your riding skill but aren't nearly so confident about what is expected of you. And you've heard hunts are rather strict. Well, to answer your questions, yes, hunts are strict, and a great deal is expected of you. Let's start at the beginning; I think you'll understand why.

Most hunts in this country fall into one of three different groups. Some hunts are subsidized by hunt clubs and those who hunt must be a member of that club. Other hunts are organized by one person who is almost always the Master and people hunt solely at his (or her) invitation. The third, and probably the most popular form of a hunt today, is the subscription pack, where members are charged a certain fee per season in return for the privilege of hunting. A standard "capping fee" is charged to those who hunt only a few times and are not official members of the hunt. The phrase "capping fee" stems from the old days when a Master used to pass his cap around to everyone in the hunt field for donations to help keep his hunt going. Hunting today, even as it was in those days, is no small expense. Perhaps that's why hunting people have been affectionately referred to as the "Mink and Manure Set."

Most hunts have a hunt committee whose purpose is to think of ways to make money for the hunt. Hunt committees produce horse shows, hunter trials (horse shows specifically designed for horses that hunt), fairs, horse races, hound races, and everything else they can dream up to make money to enable their hunt to function successfully. It is an honor to be asked to serve on a hunt committee, although after a while no one on the committee is sure why. Hunt-committee members work long and hard for the sport they love.

The formal hunting season starts about the time the young fox cubs have grown up enough to be hunted fairly by a foxhound. The two most common breeds of foxhounds hunted in this country are the American Foxhound and the English Foxhound. Fox hunters have an extensive vocabulary peculiar to their sport. For instance, a foxhound is *never* called a dog. He is a foxhound or he may be referred to simply as "hound." Any other dog seen while hunting is referred to as a cur. So if you have a friend who's come out on foot to watch the hunt and he's brought along his purebred, very expensive poodle, don't be upset when the master calls out a warning to his Huntsman to "keep my hounds away from that cur!" He really doesn't mean it personally. It's hunting vernacular.

The end of September or first part of October is the date most hunts choose to open. Before formal hunting starts, however, there is a period of time in the late summer and early fall when cub hunting is in effect. Cub hunting serves several purposes, the major one being to introduce the young hounds into a hunting atmosphere.

All summer long, the young hounds have been hound-walked and trained to listen to the Huntsman. Each pup starts out by being tied by the collar (coupled) to an older, more experienced hound. Huntsmen find it easier to count the hounds by twos; thus a hunt identifies its hounds by saying they have, for example, 14½ couple (or 29 hounds). Finally, however, the time comes when the young hounds must be released to see how well they'll do on their own. Thus, cub hunting begins.

The hunt is usually slow and the hounds are worked carefully. If a young fox is found, he is encouraged to run but is rarely killed. Cub hunting is lesson time. This is also an excellent time to introduce a new horse to the hunt field, to introduce a novice fox hunter to hunting, or to show an experienced fox hunter new country that has just been "opened." Attire is informal and the hunt is relaxed. By the time formal hunting begins, the hounds have learned their job, the fox has learned to run, and the "Season of the Real Chase" begins. It continues as long as weather permits hound to hunt safely and horse and rider to travel safely.

Unfortunately today's hunt has many problems. The bane of any fox-hunting group is the hunter on foot who lies in wait for the hounds to find a fox and then shoots him as he starts to run. He's not only ruined a good chase for those mounted on horseback but, even worse, he has not allowed the fox a sporting chance to survive. In fox hunting it is only animal against animal. We humans do nothing but follow the hounds that follow the fox.

Hunt country is constantly being swallowed by civilization. Many lovely farms have been subdivided and built upon and some hunts have died already because of lack of land. Others have resorted to drag hunting in order to survive. (In a drag hunt, the hounds and field follow a specific trail that has been carefully laid with fox scent ahead of time.)

The hounds, whether the hunt be live or drag, are in constant danger from the all-too-rapid automobile traffic which seems to be everywhere. Then, too, homes and other civilized areas confuse the hounds and keep them from staying exclusively on fox scent. The fox, of course, is quite aware of all this and uses it to his advantage. Stories of "Reynard" eluding the hounds are legion. Some are true and some are marvelous fabrications. But they all spring from one basic fact that every fox hunter will swear to: the fox is a very clever guy.

The prime object in fox hunting is to kill the fox. A fox is, as he always has been, a plague to the farmer. He cleverly discovers all too soon that it is much easier to invade a farmyard for his dinner than to spend a lot of energy hunting for it. However, in many parts of our country, killing a fox is easier said than done. Because of civilization and because of the fox's own ingenuity, he more often escapes or runs to earth in one of the many hollow trees or other animal holes in the area. If the hounds are skillful and catch the fox, the farmer over whose land we travel is delighted and the hounds kill the fox very quickly. A gun or trap is not always so humane. Fortunately, the hound work and the chase are the most exciting parts of hunting or I'm sure the sport, in many parts of this country at least, would die almost immediately.

Not every rider is capable of hunting. It takes courage, skill, and as one friend of mine has said repeatedly, "a fox hunter must be a little bit balmy." Why else would he arrive home from a hunt covered with mud, sopping wet, tired (because he's been up since 4:00 A.M.), and still be happy and very much at peace with himself and the world?

The rider who hunts must know how to walk, trot, canter, and jump fences with a fair amount of dexterity. If the hunt is established in wooded country, the rider not only has to know how to ride and jump obstacles successfully, but how to bend himself into all sorts of contortions at speed in order to avoid being knocked on the head by low tree branches, cracked on the knees going through narrow areas, ruining his boots going through rivers and streams, or scratching his face while traveling through underbrush. Errors of judgment happen sooner or later to most of us and we find ourselves on the ground. The challenge of the terrain is always a fascinating part of fox hunting.

Don't believe that just any horse will do. A good, trustworthy horse is essential. The good fox-hunting horse knows how to travel quietly in a group and he knows how to travel intelligently and safely over his own hunt country. He may be the ugliest horse imaginable but if he can perform his work well he'll be treated with all the care and indulgence of a king. Good fox-hunting horses are not easy to find.

Never forget that the Master or Joint Masters are the people in charge and their word is *law.* Do their bidding and do it quickly. The title remains Master although the Master may be a woman. It is the Master who decides when and where each hunt will be, and he (or she) is responsible for maintaining the kennels and the hounds. The Master is assisted by the Whippers-in. I think of them as the advance patrol. They never ride with the field, but are posted to the right and left of the main field of riders where they can view the fox when he leaves a covert or decides to change direction. It is the "Whip's" duty to report his find to the Master and Huntsman. The Whippers-in also have sufficient hound knowledge to assist the Huntsman and the Master with the hounds when necessary. Sometimes the hunt includes a Field Master, which leaves the Master free to whip or ride wherever he pleases. Then the Field Master is in charge of the main group of fox hunters.

The Huntsman has a great deal of work to do, for it is up to him to take care of and to control the hounds. At the start of a meet the Huntsman sends his hounds into a covert, a patch of wood or brush where a fox is likely to be found. When they are sent into the covert, the hounds are said to "draw" the area. The Huntsman during this time encourages his hounds with his voice to "seek out." He must be careful, too, that his hounds don't spread out so far that when one of the hounds does find the scent, they cannot come together into a pack quickly. Those of you who hunt with any type of hound know how difficult that is.

It is hoped the hounds will find scent, although sometimes a young hound will speak before he is really sure he has found anything. The Huntsman recognizes all their voices and if he feels the hound who has spoken is not reliable but only showing "youthful enthusiasm," he will wait until another, wiser, more experienced hound "honors" the younger one. When that happens, the Huntsman quickly calls all his hounds together by voice and by horn. The riders in the field, hearing that special call, gather their reins in anticipation and secure their feet in their stirrups. If you're like me, the goose bumps start. I love the sound. Even the horses seem to recognize the call. And then the chase is on.

Hunting etiquette is important. Common sense and good manners are required at all times for there is always the possibility of injury either to a horse or to a rider—especially when a group of horses is traveling at high speed. Some rules are followed in order to assist the Master and the Huntsman when working the hounds. Some of the formalities are only common courtesy.

Promptness is expected. It is fact that a late rider could inadvertently upset the entire meet. Too many riders, in their hurry to catch up with the field, have unknowingly turned a fox into another direction or even crossed the fox's line of travel without knowing they have done so, thus spoiling the line of scent for the hounds. Woe be unto those riders who do "cross the line" and are caught. Sometimes, to put it mildly, a Master is not friendly at all. Watch out! Hilltoppers, those who come on foot or on horseback to watch the hunt, must be careful, also, not to interfere with the hounds or to find themselves ahead of the Huntsman.

Before the meet, the Master, Huntsman, and other members of the staff have a great deal on their minds. Don't charge forward eagerly to introduce yourself or to renew an acquaintance. Introductions and so on take place after the meet is over. The field (the group of riders who follow behind the Master) stays apart from the staff and although they may talk quietly among themselves, they leave the staff and the hounds to their work. Don't despair if no one speaks to you. They really aren't being rude. Fox hunters are a cordial group, but I personally think they like to see how you can perform in the field before they'll accept you. Prove yourself first.

The riders quietly fall in behind the Master or Field Master, usually in order of seniority, as the hunt moves out. Older, more experienced members of the hunt fall in first, then junior members, then new fox hunters and juniors who are not yet members. Top priority goes to those who have been members of the hunt for the longest time. One must earn the right to ride directly behind the Master.

However, there are no rules of riding order when a fox has been found and the chase has begun. Those riders who are the most alert, who can keep their seat, and can keep the pace will be in at the finish, whether child or adult. But never forget that pushing, shoving, or running another horse out of the way is very poor sportsmanship and not acceptable. Distance between horses is kept as usual. Jumps are met fairly and without crowding. Horses that refuse a jump must drop back until there is a fair gap in the field, at which time they may try again.

The field has a definite responsibility to the hunt. Not only does the Huntsman need quiet in order to work his hounds, but the Field Master needs quiet to translate the sounds the hounds and Huntsman make. Therefore, socializing takes place only before or after the actual hunt. Loud voices are annoying. If you are asked to keep quiet—take your scolding and learn from it. New offenders are forgiven. Constant offenders won't be invited back.

The field follows the hounds, never goes before the hounds. Hounds have the right of way at all times. Any horse that kicks at a hound will not be tolerated. After all, no hounds, no hunt!

No member of the staff should be crowded at any time. If the Master and the staff find they must double back, the field backs out of the way, always facing their horses toward the Master and staff. The Master and staff may find the opportunity sometime during the hunt to formally greet the field. Again, riders, always face toward the Master. Don't let the Master's smile fool you. He is really inspecting his hunt. Make very sure you and your horse are attired correctly.

The gentleman who dismounts to hold a gate open for the field to pass through is a boon to any hunt and his considerate action is duly noted by the Master. No more than one or two riders should remain behind until the gateman is back in his saddle again. They ensure the gateman's safety.

The same procedure is followed when a rider falls. One or two riders should remain to retrieve the horse and assist the rider. The other riders should continue on. Thus the main body of the hunt is never broken and people are not lost and/or strewn over the countryside to wander on property they have no business riding on or to spoil the hunt for others.

Riders in the field should always be alert to straggler hounds coming up from behind. They should also be on the lookout for deep holes or other possible dangers. The proper call if you find something dangerous is "Ware hound" (hole, wire, etc.), and because hearing is poor when a number of horses are galloping, point your finger toward the danger area.

Horses new to fox hunting should always remain at the back of the field. Even the quietest horse can put up quite a fuss when he's suddenly placed into a situation he doesn't understand. Our Sam was the world's worst offender. He reared, he bolted fences, he jigged and jogged for hours on end. I couldn't believe the difference in him. I think it was only blind faith that his inherent quietness would eventually come forth that made me continue hunting him. It certainly wasn't anything else. But the day finally came. How proud I was when he learned to stand quietly at a check; to walk, trot, canter, and jump at *my* command—not his whimsy. For me, he became a real Cadillac in the hunt field.

One of the most important responsibilities of the field is to respect and take care of the land over which the hunt rides. Keep the land clean. Keep trash in your pockets or in the sandwich bag. If a member of the staff asks riders to stay out of a field, he means it! Please honor his request. The hunt that respects landowners' property, reports any damage to the staff as quickly as possible, and is friendly and pleasant to each and every person it sees is the hunt that will continue to be allowed to hunt over that property.

Riders should ride through farmyards no faster than at a slow trot. Be on a constant lookout for stray chickens, ducks, pigs, and children that may dart out from just about anywhere at any time. Be very, very careful, not just because you might run over someone or something, but because your horse can take real issue over strange animals. You may know that that four-legged creature is a pig, but I'll wager your horse won't, at least not at first, especially if the pig decides to squeal. Keep alert and you'll remain in the saddle.

Don't disappear immediately after the hunt until you've thanked your Master for the hunt even if it's been a blank day (no fox was found). Don't be shy. Introduce yourself if you are alone. If the hunt is a subscription pack, money should be left with the Field Secretary or, at the least, your name, address, and phone number so you can be billed later.

If a hound is missing, stay a while longer if you have the time. The Master and the Huntsman are usually grateful for a little company, and an extra pair of eyes is always helpful. It's a lonely time. The Huntsman stands and calls and calls and calls on the horn for his hound to come in. The Master paces, looks, and listens. Finally, if they're lucky, the hound returns in good health. Sometimes they're not so lucky and the hound comes in slowly and in great pain. The pain is seen in the Master's and the Huntsman's eyes, too. We can only hope and pray he will survive. Foxhounds are a valiant breed. Many, because of their own persistent hunting instincts, have unwittingly harmed themselves in pursuit of their quarry. The Master and his staff try their best to protect them but, as we have all discovered, accidents happen.

Correct hunting attire is important, not only because with uniform attire the group becomes a dignified and impressive-looking whole, but because, for the most part, there is a good reason for every piece of clothing one wears.

Landowners and other onlookers do see a lovely and—let's face it—a romantic picture when members of the hunt ride by immaculately and formally attired. The effect is neat, exciting, and somehow—permissible. A group of slovenly, unkempt riders on dirty horses will always make an undesirable picture and the inclination of any landowner would automatically be to refuse the group access to his property. Who could blame him?

Of course, there is a reason for the attire other than the picture it presents. A black coat does not show the dirt as quickly as any bright color will and the black has the added advantage of blending into the countryside. The white stock becomes a very useful sling or bandage in the event of an accident. The stock pin (a rather glorified gold safety pin) is a far

Formal Hunt or Show Attire

better means to secure a bandage than a less solid trinket from a jewelry store. Hunting is usually done when the weather is cold and/or damp. A vest provides added warmth and protection. Gloves are used for warmth but they also prevent fingers from slipping on leather reins when the weather is wet. High leather boots are a necessity, for without them breeches might be torn and legs scratched and cut as riders travel through underbrush. The derby is worn for two reasons. Its hard casing protects the rider in case of a fall and the brim is useful to deflect brush from the face and to keep rain from dripping down the back of one's neck. There is a cord hat guard that connects the hat to a button or loop on the back of the riding jacket. Most times the cord is not necessary at all, but use it anyway. I have seen an unruly horse buck so hard that the derby was finally dislodged from his rider's head, and I have seen other times when riders who were careless and didn't take the time to fasten their derbies lose the hunt because their hats fell off and they had to backtrack to retrieve them. Much better to connect the cord and have the derby on hand at all times. Keep your Master happy!

Although it is no longer required, some people choose to wear a leather strap (garter) around the top of their boots to help keep the boots up and smooth on the leg. If the garter is worn, the buckle should face the front of the leg. If the buckle is placed on the inside of the leg, it may chafe; if placed on the outside of the leg, it may catch on a branch. Three small buttons must be sewed on the seam of the breeches above the boot. They are a vestige of the past when stretch pants were not prevalent, and breeches had to be buttoned all the way up the leg in order to fit well. The buttons provide a secure holder for the boot garter when the garter lies between the second and third buttons.

Women may choose to wear patent-leather tops on their boots, which act as a dust and grime repellent. Remember, though, patent tops are worn only with formal and very formal attire. With patent-leather tops the boot garter should be patent leather. Plain leather tops should have plain leather straps. Spurs, if worn, are placed high on the boot, usually at the seam between the shoe of the boot and the tops. Spurs that slip and slide are not effective. Spurs placed too low on the boot are not effective either.

Master and staff wear colorful attire. The scarlet or "pink coat" is worn, first, because the picture presented is lovely to look at and, second, because staff can be more easily identified from a distance. Staff wear a cap instead of a derby, because hearing is better with a cap. The cap helps onlookers to differentiate between the professional members (paid) and amateur members (nonpaid) of the staff, for hunt caps have a black ribbon encircling the base of the cap. If the ends of the ribbon at the back of the cap point down, the member is a professional. If the tabs point up, he is an amateur.

The Master designates those members of the hunt who have earned the right to wear the hunt colors. Wear them with pride. The color the hunt has selected as its own—green, yellow, crimson, or whatever—is sewed onto the collar, and buttons with the insignia of the hunt are worn on the coat. Some hunts allow only gentleman members to wear the hunt colors. Women wear only the hunt button. In other hunts both men and women may wear the collar and the button. Patent-leather tops may be permissible for men and women or they may be permissible only for women. Each hunt sets its own standards. The attire, as described, is acceptable everywhere. Do not assume that because a hunt cap or a blue or green jacket, for instance, are allowed in your hunt that they are acceptable everywhere. They are not.

Regardless of the particular requirements of each hunt, the attire is essentially the same. And because it is, any onlooker can see a group of fox hunters ride by and in a matter of minutes discern who is a member of the staff, who is professional, who is an amateur, who is a member of the hunt, who may be a guest from another hunt, and who may be a member of the field but has not yet earned the right to wear the hunt colors or button.

The horse and the rider must be neat. Obviously a well-brushed and groomed horse is going to feel better than his counterpart with burrs in

Hunt Crop and Lash

Top Hat

Stock

Shirt

Vest

"Pink" Coat

Gloves

Breeches

Boots

Very Formal Men's Hunt Attire

his mane and tail. Clean tack will not rub or chafe and it should be checked over completely before the hunt for possible frayed or broken parts. Riders (male or female) with long hair should have it neatly combed and fastened securely either by hairnets or pins under the cap or derby.

For many of us hunting has become a do-it-yourself endeavor. A word of warning if you are one of the "do-it-yourselfers": allow plenty of time to prepare for a hunt. Many hunts take place in the early-morning hours because it is the nature of the fox to do his own hunting at those hours and it's easier to find a fox when he's up and around. The early hour means that the fox hunter must make most of his preparations the night before. Tack should be cleaned (if it isn't already) and carefully checked for necessary repairs. Your horse should be carefully groomed also so that all he needs (if you're lucky!) is a once-over in the morning. Those who own their own trailer should hitch up the night before to avoid the possibility of error in the early-morning darkness and hurry. Clothes should be gathered and placed where they can be put on with all possible speed. Beware! Allow time for problems that might come up—like the horse that suddenly decides he doesn't want to go into the trailer. Oh, the stories told in the hunt field concerning early-morning emergencies! They could fill a whole book. One of my favorites was told by a friend whose horse decided one day to be one of "those who wouldn't load." It was 5:00 A.M. Johnny, beautifully and immaculately dressed for hunting, led Royal Sport into the trailer, fastened him securely, and then walked behind to close up the back. In that short amount of time, Royal decided to cause trouble. He jerked back, broke his halter, hastily backed himself out, and took off into the darkness. As my friend said later, *How* do you find a black horse in the black of night?" At any rate, after due time tramping through the mud, Johnny did find him, gave Royal a new halter, and proceeded to reload him—with the same results. Finally, in desperation, he yelled for help only to see his wife materialize sleepily out of the darkness into the barn light. She was dressed only in a pair of high boots, her nightgown, and a coat. Most important of all—sleepy though she was—she carried a broom. Once more the loading began. This time, though, Royal got a good swat on the rear with the broom, which firmly convinced him to behave. Then, as quietly as she had come, Johnny's wife disappeared back into the darkness.

The hunting horse should wear only the amount of equipment he needs to be easily controlled. No one wants a horse that won't stop quickly or turn quickly if the occasion demands it (especially as the Master will breathe *fire* if he is passed in the hunt field). A breastplate is worn if the horse's body build (conformation) is such that the saddle has a tendency to slide back from its proper position. Similarly, a crupper attached under the tail helps keep the saddle from sliding forward. Martingales can be dangerous and shouldn't be used unless absolutely necessary, the reason being that any piece of equipment that hangs from the horse may be the piece that gets caught going through a thicket. Horses that get entangled react very differently. While some stand quietly, others panic and can cause terrible harm to themselves, their riders, and even others who may try to come to their aid. Thank God for the rider who thinks to include a pair of clippers as standard riding equipment.

Van and trailer drivers can be the cause of many problems. Be careful when parking in hunt country. I know it's difficult to maneuver large vehicles, but don't run down the farmer's mailbox or his flowers, park in front of his driveway so he can't leave home, or drive on his lawn when turning around. Country roads are usually narrow. It's best to park so that other cars, trucks, and buses can get through. It may mean a longer walk for you and your horse, but the results are well worth the extra trouble. Your landowner remains happy and the school bus can squeeze through on its way to school.

Many hard-riding fox hunters are disappointed when they come upon a blank day. All they truly want is the excitement of the gallop and to "lark" over as many fences as they can. However, let's face it, sometimes the weather is poor for scenting purposes and other times the hounds find a fox that doesn't feel like running. He immediately finds a hole and goes to ground. This happens as often as not. But that, too, is part of the sport.

Duck hunters sometimes wait for hours in a duck blind. Deer hunters (several that I know, anyway) can go all day without finding a deer. Hunting fox is no different. But for those who love the sport and the horse, there is never a really bad day. It's always satisfying to be mounted and always a pleasure to be out with friends.

Leave any criticism of your Master and the Huntsman at home. After all, they want a day filled with good sport as badly as you do. And they work a lot harder for it. This may seem a little harsh, but my feeling is that if you don't like the way the hunt is being run, you should get out. No one forced you to join it.

Those with a true interest in fox hunting can make use of the blank days to listen to the Huntsman and the hounds. Watch how they work. Why did the Huntsman draw there? What is he saying to his hounds? You'll soon learn to identify the hounds and their voices. The day will come when you may find yourself shepherding a group of children way back in the field and still know which hound has spoken or which hound has found. Fox hunters have discovered that the more one comes to understand, the more fun one can have, even on a blank day.

The social life connected with hunting is very special. Whether the occasion is a group of happy riders stopping at a diner for a late breakfast or a hunt ball, the camaraderie and good feeling remain.

Most hunts offer hunt breakfasts throughout the season and they are lovely. Keep a rag and a stiff brush handy in your car to clean off all the extraneous mud and dirt you've accumulated on your ride and then present yourself with pride. If a nonriding member of your family is to join you later at the breakfast make sure that he is in coat and tie or she is in a smart-looking suit, wool dress, or a pantsuit suitably designed for dining. The breakfast itself can vary from pancakes served country style to "pheasant under glass" served formally. The bar is usually open. Don't forget that sudden warmth, good food, and alcoholic spirits can go to your head quickly after hours of vigorous exercise in the fresh air. Be careful. Especially if you still have to drive you and your horse home. Most important of all, make sure your horse is comfortable, perhaps even bandaged, and has plenty of hay to munch if he must wait for you. Don't sacrifice your horse for your pleasure.

Hunt balls are traditional, formal, and perfectly beautiful. A gentleman wears black or white tie, a woman, her loveliest gown. Gentlemen who have earned their colors may wear a set of scarlet tails with the hunt colors on the lapel especially designed for evening wear. The color and the gaiety are all impressive. It can be awesome.

I'm still amused by a friend of mine who claims he went to his first hunt ball years ago feeling very cool and confident knowing he was looking oh so swish in his white tie and tails. He felt marvelous only until he set foot in the door whereupon he saw man after man gorgeously attired in "formal red coats with those crazy colors on the lapels." He felt outclassed. But then he decided to rise to the challenge. He would "outmanner" his competition. How? He became most adept at opening doors and lighting ladies' cigarettes before the other gentlemen could get their hands out of their pockets. It wasn't long before he learned to view the "red" coats with aplomb, but his practice lighting cigarettes quickly has helped him with the ladies to this day. We're all flattered by prompt attention, aren't we?

How does one go about hunting? Fox-hunting friends are the easiest entry. It's probably best to contact the nearest hunt stable if you're new to an area and don't know anyone. The stable will direct you to the correct person (usually the Hunt Secretary), who in turn will explain the rules of entry for their particular hunt. The rider who plans to visit in a strange area and would like to hunt writes a letter of introduction to the Hunt Secretary asking permission to hunt.

It is wise to ask what the proper attire is when away from home. Every hunt has its own requirements and some hunts prefer visitors to wear the black coat minus color or buttons even though you've earned the right to wear them in your own hunt. A hunt member, of course, has the easiest entry into another hunt, especially if he thinks to include, with his own letter, a letter of introduction from his Master. Most hunts do welcome guests and can provide horses for you. The library can supply you with information on all the hunts, the type of country over which they travel, and the person to contact. Every year *The Chronicle of the Horse,* published in Middleburg, Virginia, includes a listing of all the recognized hunts with essentially the same information.

Always take your best attire whether you wish to hunt abroad or in this country. Although some hunts are not as formal as others, it would be a shame not to be able to dress correctly if the hunt requires formal attire. One can always dress "down" if the occasion demands it. It is not always so easy to dress "up." Besides that, you are representing your hunt and, believe me, your Master will hear about a poor showing.

HUNTING ATTIRE

Lady: Cub-hunting Attire

Hat:	Black derby with hat guard.
Shirt:	White shirt or ratcatcher with bow tie of same material as shirt; choker or attractive pin.
Jacket:	Any tweed or muted color preferred.
Pants:	Breeches (gray, yellow, brown) worn with high boots or jodhpurs (gray or tan) worn with jodhpur boots (brown).
Boots:	May be rubber, canvas, or leather. Black or brown.
Gloves:	Leather or string (not necessary but handy if it rains).

Gentleman: Cub-hunting Attire

Same as for lady except for shirt, which *may* be in color but more often is white and worn with a tie.

Junior: Cub-hunting Attire (to age sixteen)

Same attire as above, but juniors may wear a hunt cap.

Lady: Formal Hunting Attire

Hat:	Black derby with hat guard. A silk hat is required for very formal wear.
Shirt:	White.
Stock:	White and worn with a gold stock pin, fastened horizontally.
Jacket:	Black melton, Oxford gray, or navy blue. Black buttons. For very formal occasions black swallow tail (shad belly) or cutaway (weasel belly) are allowed.
Breeches:	Shades of gray, tan, or canary.
Vest:	Usually yellow cloth unless material is otherwise specified by the hunt.
Gloves:	Brown or tan leather. Rain gloves are white string and are carried under the girth, thumb pressed against palm of glove and against saddle, fingers facing the front of the saddle.
Boots:	Must be black leather. Women may wear black patent-leather tops. Patent-leather tops must be worn with formal wear. Tabs, located on each side of the tops, should be sewed on but not sewed down. Patent-leather boot garters may be worn with patent-leather tops. Garters go between the second and third buttons on the breeches.

Gentleman: Formal Hunting Attire

Hat:	Black derby with hat guard. Silk hat worn with very formal attire.
Shirt:	White.
Stock:	White with gold stock pin worn horizontally.
Jacket:	Black melton with black buttons. Very formal wear includes scarlet coat with brass buttons if permitted by master to wear scarlet, or swallow tail (shad belly) or cutaway (weasel belly).
Vest:	Same as for lady.

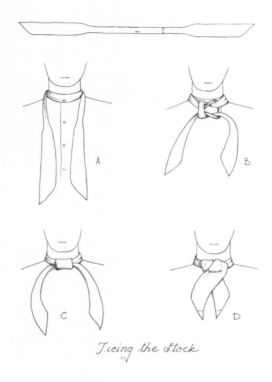

Tieing the Stock

Breeches:	Gray or brown may be worn with black coat. Scarlet attire —breeches are white.
Gloves:	Same as for lady.
Boots:	Black boots. Patent-leather tops may or may not be permissible depending upon the hunt. Don't wear them until you are sure you may. Tan tops are worn only by hunt staff or by gentlemen members wearing scarlet.

Junior: Formal Hunting Attire
Complies with lady or gentleman attire as described above. Juniors up to age sixteen may wear a black hunt cap. Some hunts do not require junior

members to wear formal wear (the black melton and white stock) until age sixteen. Juniors never wear very formal attire.

The hunting stock is not as difficult to tie as many people imagine. There are "ready-tied" stocks on the market, which are acceptable but not practical. Be brave—buy a regular stock and learn how to attach it. Be careful to buy a stock that fits your own neck.

I find the following procedure to be the easiest way to tie a stock correctly. Stocks have two buttonholes and a slit. The buttonhole in the middle of the stock buttons to the top front button on your shirt. The second buttonhole attaches to the button on the back of your shirt. The rest of the length of stock slips through the slit to make it secure and is carried around to the front of the neck. The remainder is tied in a loose square knot (right hand over left, then left hand over right). The knot is tied loosely so that the front part can be pulled out to cover the knot. Then the two ends are drawn gently over and across the knot. The tips are secured beneath your vest to the shirt by two small safety pins. The knot itself and the two crossed ends are firmly attached by a gold safety pin placed horizontally so that if the pin does come undone, the rider is not stabbed in the neck! Some pins become dull with time. Stick the point in a bar of soap now and then. It helps to prevent dulling.

Hunting Glossary

Appointments: Proper attire of both horse and rider.

Away: When a fox leaves his covert he has "gone away." Hounds that follow the fox out of the covert have "gone away."

Babble: A hound that speaks for any reason other than to acknowlege scent of the fox is said to "babble."

Billet: Fox excrement.

Bitch: Female hound.

Blank: A hunting day on which no fox is found is called a "blank day." One covert may turn out to be a "blank draw."

Brush: Tail of the fox.

Breast high and burning scent: When scent is so clear ("breast high") that hounds do not have to drop their heads to find it, hounds will run at a very fast pace and will often run mute. Drag-hunting hounds may run mute because of "burning scent" (strong scent on the ground).

Burst: A portion of the run that is particularly fast.

Bye day: Any extra hunting day that has not been previously scheduled on the hunt calendar.

Cap: A hard, black, tight-fitting cap with a narrow visor worn by hunting staff and children under the age of sixteen. In some hunts, people who are not regular members of the hunt are asked to pay a "cap fee" for the privilege of hunting that day.

Cast: Hounds that have been set loose by the Huntsman to find a fox.

Check: Any time the forward motion of the hunt stops (such as when hounds lose the line of scent), there is a check.

Cold scent: Any scent that is difficult or almost impossible for hounds to follow.

Colors: Each hunt chooses its own colors and is identified by them. When a member of the hunt earns his colors, he is entitled to wear the hunt color on his coat collar along with other apparel particular to that hunt—for instance, coat buttons bearing the insignia of the hunt and vest made of a specially designed material.

Couple: Hounds are always counted in couples: 12½ couple = 25 hounds.

Covert (pronounced "cover"): Any wooded or overgrown area where a fox is likely to be found.

Crop: The stiff part of a hunting whip. Any stiff bat used as an artificial aid for the horse.

Cry: The sounds hounds make when hunting.

Cub: A young fox.

Cub hunting: The informal hunting that takes place before the formal hunting season begins. The purpose of cub hunting is to train young fox cubs to break from covert and run, train young horses to hunt, and to introduce young hounds to the hunt.

Cur: Any dog—even a purebred—the hunt comes across other than its own hounds.

Dew claw: The false toe and claw found on hounds' forelegs.

Dog fox: A male fox.

Dog hound: A male hound.

Downwind: Hounds may run downwind, that is, with the wind behind them.

Drag hunt: A type of hunt in which hounds follow a line of scent specially prepared for them in advance.

Draw: The hounds' being sent by the Huntsman to search for a fox in a covert is called a "draw."

Double back: The fox that returns to the covert in which he was originally found is said to "double back."

Earth: The place where a fox goes into the ground.

Feathering: A hound "feathers" by waving his stern (tail), indicating interest but not yet enthusiasm for the line of scent.

Field: Hunt followers who are not members of the staff.

Field Master: The person designated to control and direct the field.

Fixture: A fixture card designating times and dates of each meet, which is sent to each hunt member.

Gone to ground: A fox that seeks cover in the earth is said to have "gone to ground."

Head: A fox traveling in one direction but then forced by outside influences to turn is said to have been "headed."

Heel: Hounds that find a line of scent but run it backward are said to be running a "heel" line.

Hold hard: A phrase meaning to stop immediately, no matter at what rate of speed your horse may be traveling.

Honor: When a hound speaks and thus backs up another hound that has found scent, the hound is said to have "honored" it.

Huntsman: The person designated to take care of and hunt the hounds.

Kennels: The place where hounds live.

Lark: To jump fences unnecessarily.

Lift: Hounds are "lifted" when the Huntsman removes them from a cold line to draw another covert.

Line: The track made by the fox.

Litter: A group of young born of the same mother.

Livery: Special clothes worn by the Master and his staff.

Mark: A hound that indicates by either digging or speaking in a special way is "marking" the ground where the fox has gone to ground.

Mask: The head of the fox.

Master: The man or woman in command of the kennels, the hounds, and our good sport.

Music: The cry of the pack.

Mute: Hounds that follow the line of scent without speaking are said to be "running mute."

Nose: The ability of a hound to detect scent.

Open: When a hound first gives tongue, he is said to "open."

Pad: The foot of a fox.

Pink: The scarlet livery worn by the hunt staff, called "Pink" after the tailor named Pink who originated it.

Put down: To put to death.

Quarry: The hunted animal.

Rack: A way through a fence.

Ratcatcher: The name applied to the shirt most often worn with informal riding attire. It has a long tie, which is worn in the form of a bow tie at the rider's neck.

Riot: When hounds hunt deer or anything other than fox they are said to "riot."

Run: The chase.

Scent: The odor given off by the fox.

Speak: When a hound gives tongue, he is "speaking."

Staff: Huntsman, Whippers-in, and Field Master.

Stern: A hound's tail.

"Tally Ho": The cry when one sees a fox.

Tongue: The cry of the hound. A hound gives "tongue" when he notifies the Huntsman by voice that he has found the line.

Uniform: The dress worn by members of the field.

"View Holloa": The cry spoken by staff when a fox is viewed.

Vixen: A female fox.

Ware: Short for "beware." "Ware hole," "ware wire," and so on.

Whelp: A young puppy.

Whipper-in: A staff member who assists the Huntsman in the control of the hounds.

Young entry: Young hounds. Young riders in the field.

Photo Credits

Index